AN ILLUSTRAT

WEAPONS OF THE
SPECIAL FORCES

AN ILLUSTRATED GUIDE TO

WEAPONS OF THE

SPECIAL FORCES

Max Walmer

An Arco Military Book

Prentice Hall Press

New York London Toronto Sydney Tokyo

Prentice Hall Press
Gulf + Western Building
One Gulf + Western Plaza
New York, New York 10023

Copyright © 1989 by Salamander Books Ltd.

An Arco Military Book

PRENTICE HALL PRESS and colophon are registered
trademarks of Simon & Schuster Inc.

Originally published in 1989 in the United Kingdom by
Salamander Books Ltd., 52 Bedford Row, London WC1R 4LR.

This book may not be sold outside the United States
of America and Canada.

Library of Congress Cataloging-in-Publication Data

Walmer, Max.
   An illustrated guide to weapons of the special forces.
   1. Firearms. 2. Special forces (Military science) —
Equipment and supplies. I. Title.
UD380.W35   1989   623.4'4   88-36246
ISBN 0-13-451048-8

Credits

Author: Max Walmer is a British Officer who has had considerable service
in Malaya, the Falklands, Europe and other areas. He has written many
military books and technical articles on defense affairs.

Editor: Linda Jones
Designed by: Philip Gorton and Paul Johnson
Artworks: Terry Hadler and Geoff Denney
Filmset by: The Old Mill
Color reproduction by: Magnum Graphics Ltd
Printed: in Belgium by Proost International Book Production, Turnhout.

Photographs: The publisher wishes to thank all the official government
archives and individuals who have supplied pictures for this book.

10 9 8 7 6 5 4 3 2 1
First Prentice Hall Press Edition

Contents

Introduction   8

WEAPONS
Pistols:
9mm Heckler & Koch P7M8   14
9mm Heckler & Koch P9S   15
Sub-machine guns:
9mm Heckler & Koch MP5   16
9mm MAT 49   20
9mm UZI/Mini-UZI/Micro-UZI   22
9mm L34A1 Sterling silenced   24
9mm Ingram Models 10/11   26
5.45mm AKR   28
Rifles:
5.56mm SR88   30
5.56mm FA MAS   32
5.56mm & 7.62mm Galil   36
5.56mm AR 70/223 Beretta   38
5.45mm AK-74 and AKS-74   40
7.62mm AK-47 and AKM   42
5.56mm Colt Commando   44
5.56mm M16A1/A2   46
Sniper rifles:
7.62mm Accuracy International Model PM   48
7.62mm Heckler & Koch PSG1   50
7.62mm Heckler & Koch G3SG/1   52
7.62mm Dragunov (SVD)   54
Shotguns:
12-bore Franchi SPAS 12   56
12-bore Ithaca 37   58
12-bore Mossberg 500 ATP8   58
37mm ARWEN 37   60
70mm ARMSEL Striker   62
Light machine guns:
5.56mm M249 Squad Automatic Weapon (SAW)   64
7.62mm L7A2   66
7.62mm PK series   68
Rocket launchers:
RPG series   70
LAW80 light anti-tank weapon   74
Surface-to-air missile launchers:
Stinger, FIM-92A   76
Blowpipe/Javelin   78
SA-7 Grail   80

TECHNOLOGY
Operations   82
Ammunition   92
Silenced weapons   98
Grenades   102
Exotic weapons, equipment and uniforms   106
Sensors   112
Communications   114
Vehicles   116

VIRTUALLY every country today has a special force unit, specially selected and trained to a high degree of physical and mental fitness. They are kept at a high state of readiness to deal rapidly and effectively with the unexpected. These units may be used for special operations in a conventional war setting, for anti-terrorist operations (for example, to free hostages in a kidnap), or for operations in support of the civil police against increasingly sophisticated criminals, such as, for example, the use of US military units in the fight against drug smugglers.

This extraordinary breadth of possibilities means that special force units must have at their disposal a very wide range of weapons and equipment, ranging from standard military issue to special 'one-offs' developed for a particular operational need. Further, such units need to train on almost any weapon in the world. Most units keep small stocks of a variety of foreign weapons, both those which are used by friendly

forces and those used by potential enemies. Any weapon in any field is a likely candidate for use by special forces around the world; for the purposes of this book, however, we have carefully selected those which are typical in their field.

The first requirement in selecting a weapon is to establish precisely what is needed to accomplish a particular mission. If the job is to clear hallways, for example, the weapon is likely to be a shotgun, a P7 pistol or a sub-machine gun (SMG) rather than a 5.56mm or, worse, a 7.62mm service rifle. If the situation involves terrorists with multiple hostages in adjacent rooms, the choice might even center on the most suitable type of ammunition. The required end effect must be gauged; is it required to kill the target, to wound or to deter without actually hitting? Also, will a clear, well-judged shot be possible, or will it be a snatched shot taking advantage of a fleeting glimpse? Will the engagement take place in daylight, poor or artificial light, or in the

Left: Members of the French counter-terrorist group GIGN display a range of weapons needed for their mission.

Diver
1 Breathing apparatus 2 Parachute
3 Distress flare 4 Depth gauge
5 Compass 6 UZI SMG
7 Propulsion unit

Night marksman
8 Protective waistcoat 9 Odelf image intensifier 10 H&K MP5 silenced SMG 11 Laser spot projector

Gas equipment
12 Smith & Wesson 37mm grenade thrower 13 Hand-held CS grenades
14 Tear gas spray 15 Protective waistcoat 16 Gas mask

Parachutist
17 Helmet 18 Goggles 19 Back parachute 20 Front parachute
21 Altimeter 22 H&K short SMG
23 Torches 24 Reflective gaiters
25 Flying suit 26 Parachute boots

Marksman
27 Radio headset 28 FRFI sniping rifle 29 Sopolem OB50 vision device
30 Laser sight

A Climbing ropes B Colt Trooper .357 Magnum with laser C Sopolem OB44 night sight D CS gas grenades E Hand-thrown CS grenades F Manurhin revolver with optical sight G Attack grenade H Ruggieri blinding grenade I 5 litre portable CS gas dispenser J Helmet with clear visor

dark? Most of these questions cannot be answered in advance of the incident, so one of the primary requirements for a special force is as good a selection of weapons, ammunition and sights as possible.

One of the leading requirements for any weapon is a very high degree of reliability. Every weapon should work first time, every time; when a hit-team dashes into a room containing hostages and terrorists there is no scope at all for an SMG to misfire or for a grenade to fail to detonate. In addition, the weapons have to be small, sometimes small enough to be hidden in an attaché case or under a raincoat.

Weapons need to be accurate and have predictable behaviour. Modern conditions place troops and police in situations where they have to deal with terrorists, agitators or just plain criminals who deliberately surround themselves with innocent people. Weapons of the greatest precision and accuracy are needed, enabling marksmen to take out targets standing within inches of others who must not be harmed.

For specialist weapons, the special force units look first to their national resources and to the standard issue weapons of their armies. However, these weapons are often too large, too heavy, too unwieldly, too inaccurate or otherwise unsuitable, and the next option is to seek nationally produced special weapons designed

Below: US soldier checking on Soviet weapons captured in Grenada. Such weapons are widely available to terrorists.

to meet the unit's operational requirements. A fairly recent development, however, is the readiness of special force units to put aside national considerations and purchase foreign weapons, even when their own arms industry can produce something generally similar. Thus, for example, many Western countries with their own weapons industries still use the Israeli UZI or the West German Heckler & Koch MP5 SMGs.

Apart from their specialist roles special forces also take part in more conventional operations requiring conventional infantry weapons. There is less scope for the esoteric, especially in the heavier weapons; there are few alternatives where machine guns, anti-tank weapons and air defence missiles are concerned.

The basic weapon of any special force remains the rifle. In the 1950s there was a universal move away from bolt-action weapons, mostly of 0.303in or 7.92mm calibre, to 7.62mm automatic or semi-automatic rifles, such as the Belgian FN FAL, US M14 and Soviet AK-47. These weapons, however much better than their predecessors, have proved too heavy and too complicated for today's conditions, particularly as most infantry tend to move either in crowded armored personnel carriers, helicopters or aircraft, where space is at a premium. Further, the 7.62mm round was considered too heavy, especially as the widespread use of automatic and semi-automatic weapons led to vast increases in firing rates, not only straining logistic systems but also increasing the burden on the already heavily laden infantryman. There has, therefore, been a further move, this time to much smaller calibers — 5.56mm in the West and 5.45mm in the Soviet bloc.

As re-equipment with the new range of 5.56mm and 5.47mm weapons gathers pace there is increasing evidence that the next generation of weapons could be very different. The weapons are likely to use quite new types of ammunition, such as the US 4.32mm sabotted caseless round. Also, the whole weapon itself may well look quite unlike the rifle as we know it today — the Heckler & Koch G11, for example, looks more like a slim violin case than a rifle.

Special forces units, with their need for small, handy, close-range weapons have frequently in the past turned to the SMG in preference to the rifle. World War II commando units, for example, were characterised by the Thompson, Sten, US M3 or Soviet PPS-43. Such weapons were certainly light and easy to use; they were also highly inaccurate (except at the closest possible quarters), frequently unreliable and dangerously unsafe. Also, because they almost invariably used blow-back systems, their rounds had short range and poor stopping power.

There was a school of thought in

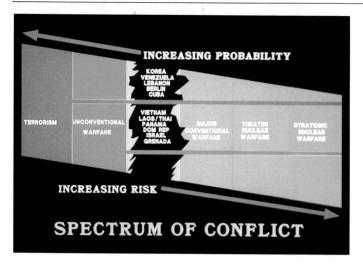

INCREASING PROBABILITY

KOREA
VENEZUELA
LEBANON
BERLIN
CUBA

VIETNAM
LAOS/THAI
PANAMA
DOM REP
ISRAEL
GRENADA

TERRORISM | UNCONVENTIONAL WARFARE | MAJOR CONVENTIONAL WARFARE | THEATER NUCLEAR WARFARE | STRATEGIC NUCLEAR WARFARE

INCREASING RISK

SPECTRUM OF CONFLICT

the 1970s which postulated that the new generation of 5.56mm rifles would be so small, light and handy that they would render the SMG obsolete. Undoubtedly as the SMG has become more sophisticated there has been a degree of convergence between its characteristics and those of the rifle, but the two have yet to meet. Indeed, in many respects the modern 5.56mm rifle is simply too powerful for the very close-quarter role in which most special force units now specialise. Thus, there is a modern range of very effective and efficient SMGs, such as the West German Heckler & Koch MP5 and the Israeli UZI. These are small, handy and have a high rate of fire; with few exceptions they fire the 9mm Parabellum round. However, some new calibers are starting to appear, such as 5.45mm in the Soviet AKR 45 and 5.56mm in the West German HK 53.

If there has been a degree of convergence between the rifle and SMG at one end of the small arms spectrum, there has been an even greater one at the other end, where some SMGs are now only a little larger than pistols. For example, the Heckler & Koch MP5K SMG is 12.8in (325mm) long and weighs 4.4lb (2kg) empty, while the archetypal pistol, the Browning, is 7.9in (200mm) long and weighs 1.8lb (0.81kg). Nevertheless, the pistol still retains its value

Above: As conflicts to the left of the spectrum become more probable governments will need special forces more than ever.

for clandestine use, being easy to hide and fire, although — despite what is depicted on TV — it is extremely difficult to use accurately over about 25yd (23m).

After a period when sniper rifles seemed to go out of fashion they are now very much back in business and apart from a few adaptations of existing service rifles there is an increasing number of specially designed weapons. Thus the British-made Accuracy International L96A1 and the Soviet Dragunov SVD sniper rifles are each unique designs, bearing no relation to any other rifles in their national inventories.

Shotguns, once the province of the sportsman, are now firmly also in the military environment. The British Army fighting in the Malayan Emergency in the 1950s found that shotguns were extremely valuable in close-range jungle ambushes, Savage 12-bore repeaters being particularly highly regarded. Today the requirement is again for a close-quarter weapon firing a large number of pellets over short ranges, but military and police requirements have led to specially designed weapons rather than simply using sporting designs. The Italian Franchi

SPAS, for example, is a rugged weapon which fires four rounds per second, enabling a trained shot to put 48 pellets a second onto a 3 x 3ft (1 x 1m) target at a range of 44yd (40m).

A new breed of weaponry which has appeared in the past decade is the specialist anti-riot gun, firing either grenades or special rounds such as batons. These exist in both single-shot and repeater versions and are used by both police and military units.

Finally, what of the weapons available to terrorist and insurgent movements? Such weapons used to be simple, frequently very ancient and sometimes home-made; indeed, in some campaigns they were notoriously unreliable and often as dangerous to the user as to the target. Today, however, terrorist movements frequently have access to the most sophisticated and modern weapons. The mujahideen in Afghanistan, for example, use the British Blowpipe and US Stinger surface-to-air missiles, while the PIRA in Northern Ireland have

managed to obtain at least a few US M16 rifles and M60 light machine guns, as well as Soviet RPG-7 rocket launchers and a variety of electronic devices, most obtained through Libya. There is also a vast stock of ex-US weapons around, abandoned in Vietnam and redistributed by the North Vietnamese; doubtless, there will soon be even more Soviet equipment on the world's arms markets being sold off by Afghanistan from stocks abandoned by the Soviet Army. Most governments, both Western and Eastern, are gradually realising that it is in the interests of all but the terrorist to restrict the wide supply of weapons beyond use by military forces. The unresolved problem is — how? And even if responsible efforts are successful, there is still scope for home-made weapons, as shown by the PIRA 'mortars' made from gas cylinders and mounted on old lorry chassis.

Below: Troopers of Federal Germany's élite Border Police unit, GSG-9, train to rescue hostages from a building.

9mm Heckler & Koch P7M8 pistol

Origin: Federal Republic of Germany. **Type:** Pistol. **Dimensions:** Length 6.8in (171mm); height 5.1in (128mm); barrel 4.2in (105mm). **Weights:** Filled magazine 2lb 1oz (950g); without magazine 1lb 11oz (780g). **Caliber:** 9mm x 19 Parabellum. **Feed:** 8-round box magazine. **Muzzle velocity:** 1,155f/s (350m/s).

Heckler & Koch's P7 has the most radically new design of recent German service pistols. Its gas-retarded blow-back operating mechanism is the same idea that was used in the World War II German *Volksturmgewehr* (VG1-5) and in an experimental Swiss self-loading pistol developed during that same era. Cocking the P7 is accomplished by squeezing the cocking lever, which runs the full length of the forward portion of the pistol-grip, instead of the conventional double-action trigger.

The P7M8 is one of two distinct versions of the P7K3 pistol, the other being the P7M13. The former holds 8 rounds in the magazine, the latter 13 — meaning there are minor changes in the frame. The P7M8 pistol is a recoil-operated weapon with a gas-retarded inertia bolt. The grip and slide are made of high-grade steel and case hardened. The fixed barrel is firmly pressed into the hardened steel grip. The barrel's polygonal profile and chamber are manufactured in one process by the cold forging method. The sight radius of 5.7in (147mm) is especially long; the height of the sight line above the firing hand is only about 1.25in (32mm).

The handy shape of the grip and the well balanced center of gravity with the very small distance of barrel axis and firing hand — only about ½ in (15mm) — result in positive behaviour of the weapon when it is fired. The grip has an ergonomically ideal angle of 110 degrees to the barrel. When the operator aims the pistol, he will instinctively use the pistol as an extension of his arm and point it at the target.

The magazine is placed almost vertically to the barrel. This guarantees optimum feed of the cartridges from the magazine to the chamber, so that jams are less likely.

The pistol is currently in use with West German Army and police units, as well as with military and police forces in other nations.

Below: P7M8 pistol with the slide held open by an empty magazine. The cocking lever can be seen at the front of the pistol grip.

9mm Heckler & Koch P9S pistol

Origin: Federal Republic of Germany. **Type:** Self-loading pistol.
Dimensions: Pistol length 7.68in (192mm); barrel length 4.08in (102mm).
Weights: 9mm pistol (empty) 1.9lb (0.88kg), (loaded) 2.34lb (1.065kg);
magazine (empty) 0.16lb (0.074kg), (loaded) 0.40lb (0.18kg). 45 ACP
(empty) 1.65lb (0.75kg), (loaded) 2.2lb (1.01kg); magazine (empty) 0.147lb
(0.067kg), (loaded) 0.48lb (0.22kg). **Cartridge:** 9mm x 19 Parabellum or .45
ACP. **Feed:** 9mm, 9-round box magazine; .45 ACP, 7-round box magazine.
Muzzle velocity: 9mm, 386f/s (351m/s); .45 ACP, 286f/s (260m/s).

In the late 1960s, Heckler & Koch of Oberndorf-Neckar, Federal Republic of
Germany, began to take a hard look at military pistols. By 1972 the company
had announced its P9S, which adapted the roller-locked bolt of its G3 rifle to
the configuration of a reliable delayed blow-back system of operation.

There seems to be little doubt that the P9S can be considered the first in a
true new generation of military handguns; its roots clearly lay in the need
during the 1970s for a modern pistol for use in counterterrorist operations,
which were on the increase, especially in Western Europe.

The P9S has a concealed double-action hammer, with an indicator pin
which protrudes when the hammer is cocked, and a hammer decocking lever
in the right front of the butt grip.

The trigger is released and the safety catch applied, with the result that the
pistol can now be holstered and carried in safety. To fire, all that is needed is to
release the safety and pull the trigger; alternatively, the decocking lever can be
pressed down to cock the hammer and allow a single-action first shot for
accuracy, should time permit this.

The P9S pistol has polygonal rifling, which — it is claimed — helps reduce
the deformation of the bullet, thus increasing the muzzle velocity. A lack of
corners at the bottom of the grooves means less accumulation of fouling and
an improvement in both accuracy and the ease of maintenance.

The P9S was adopted by the West German Border Police, which has
responsibility for the crack GSG 9 forces. It has also been adopted by various
unnamed armies and several police forces in many countries. It is available in
the United States in .45 caliber and in special long-barreled target versions.

**Below: The white spot indicates that this P9S pistol is set at 'Safe'.
This model is used by many military and police forces.**

9mm Heckler & Koch MP5

Origin: Federal Republic of Germany. **Type:** Sub-machine gun.
Dimensions: Barrel (MP5A2) 9in (225mm), (MP5A3) 9in (225mm),
(MP5SD1) 6in (146mm), (MP5SD2) 6in (146mm), (MP5SD3) 6in (146mm),
(MP5K) 5in (115mm); overall length (MP5A2) 26.8in (680mm), (MP5A3)
19.3in (490mm), (MP5SD1) 21.7in (550mm), (MP5SD2) 30.4in (780mm),
(MP5SD3) 24in (610mm), (MP5K) 12.8in (325mm). **Weights:** (MP5A2)
5.6lb (2.5kg), (MP5A3) 6.3lb (2.9kg), (MP5SD1) 6.2lb (2.9kg), (MP5SD2)
6.8lb (3.1kg), (MP5SD3) 7.5lb (3.4kg), (MP5K) 4.4lb (2kg). **Caliber:** 9mm x
19 Parabellum. **Feed:** 15/30-round box magazine. **Muzzle velocity:**
(MP5A2) 1,320f/s (400m/s), (MP5SD) 935f/s (285m/s), (MP5S) 230f/s
(375m/s). **Rate of fire:** (MP5A2) 800rpm, (MP5A3) 800rpm, (MP5SD1)
800rpm, (MP5SD2) 800rpm (MP5SD3) 800rpm, (MP5K) 900rpm. **Sights:**
Rear, four operative rotating barrel; front, hooded blade, non-adjustable.

Below: One of the truly great weapons of the current era, the 9mm
Heckler & Koch MP5 sub-machine gun, seen here in its A3 version,
is used by many special forces around the world, including the SAS.

Since its introduction in the 1960s, Heckler & Koch's MP5 has enjoyed a reputation as a weapon sophisticated enough to satisfy the requirements of the world's most elite military and police units — the British SAS and Metropolitan Police, for example. Using the same roller-delayed blowback-operating principle as its bigger brothers the G3 and C41, the MP5 features good handling qualities coupled with parts that are interchangeable with those in a wide range of heavier assault weapons.

The MP5 fires in one of three modes; semi-auto, full auto or three-, four-, or five-round burst — all of which are controlled by the trigger mechanism. Similar to the FN FAL, the H&K's safety acts as its fire selector.

Bursts are accomplished through a small ratchet "counting mechanism" interacting with the sear. Each time the bolt cycles to the rear, the ratchet advances one notch until the third, fourth or fifth cycle allows reengagement of the sear or the trigger is released, circumventing the "counter" and ending the cycle before the next shot is fired. The number of shots in the burst is determined at the time of manufacture of the trigger mechanism; it cannot therefore be varied by the firer.

These arms have great appeal to Third World countries, not only for their reliability and maintainability but also for their ease of manufacture. H&K utilizes metal stampings and welded sub-group-parts. The receiver, constructed of stamped sheet steel in 19 operations (several combined), is attached to the polygonal rifled barrel by a trunnion which is spot welded to the receiver and pinned to the barrel. The trigger housing, butt-stock and fore-

end are high impact plastic.

The MP5 has an impressive list of accessories. These include: a magazine loader, a .22 cal conversion kit; a blank firing device; a muzzle-mounted tear gas grenade launcher; and various optical devices. The MP5 has several configurations. The MP5A2 has a fixed butt-stock and the MP5A3 features a retractable stock — they are interchangeable.

The MP5K was introduced in 1976 and is designed for a special operations; the barrel is shorter, a vertical foregrip added and the rear sight apertures

Below: 9mm H&K MP5 SD6 is a silenced version with a 30-round magazine, retracting butt-stock and a 3-round burst facility.

replaced with open notches. There is no butt-stock, only a receiver cap. With an overall length of 12.8in (325mm) it fits easily into attache cases or under jackets or topcoats.

The MP5SD is a silenced weapon and identical to the MP5A2/A3 with regard to functioning principle and bolt system. MP5SD1 is the weapon with receiver cap; SD2, weapon with a fixed stock; and SD3, weapon with retractable stock. The primary feature of the silenced version is that it fires below the speed of sound, thus preventing bullet blast.

Left: MP5 SD2 with a fixed butt-stock and a 15-round magazine. An optical sight can supplement the iron sights, as shown here.

Below: Special force soldier armed with an MP5A3 SMG with an optical sight, as well as a 9mm high power Browning pistol.

9mm MAT49

Origin: France. **Type.** Sub-machine gun. **Dimensions:** Length (stock extended) 28.8in (720mm); (stock folded) 20.2in (460mm); barrel 9.1m (228mm). **Weights:** (unloaded) 7.9lb (3.6kg); (loaded) 9.2lb (4.2kg). **Cartridge:** 9mm x 79 Parabellum. **Feed:** 32- or 20-round box magazine. **Rifling:** 4 grooves l/h. **Muzzle velocity:** 1,287f/s (390m/s). **Rate of fire:** (cyclic) 600rpm.

The MAT49 sub-machine gun, which was built by Tulle (Manufacture d'Armes de Tulle), has a good reputation among French troops. First adopted by the French Army in 1949, it saw considerable service in Indochina and Algeria. A large number of these weapons, incidentally, were captured in Indochina and later converted to the Soviet 7.76mm Type P round, and the

cyclic rate was increased to 900 rounds per minute. These weapons can be recognized by their longer barrel and 35-round magazine.

Of conventional blowback design, the MAT49 has several unusual, but useful, features. The magazine housing (with magazine attached), for example, may be folded forward and clipped under the barrel — and has only to be swung back and down to be used instantly. Combined with a telescopic steel stock, this feature makes the weapon particularly usable by parachute troops. A pistol-grip squeeze safety is fitted, and this prevents accidental discharge by dropping. The ejection port cover helps keep dirt out of the internal mechanism of the gun.

The 9mm MAT49 is used by French forces and the armies of many former French colonies.

Below: The MAT 49, a well-made and dependable weapon, has proved popular with the Foreign Legion. The magazine housing can be pivoted forward to lie along the underside of the barrel jacket.

9mm UZI/Mini-UZI/ Micro-UZI

Origin: Israel. **Type:** Sub-machine gun. **Dimensions:** (UZI) 25.2in (640mm); (Mini-UZI) stock-folded 14.2in (360mm), stock extended 23.7in (600mm); Micro-UZI 10in (254mm). **Weight:** (UZI) 7.7lb (3.5kg); (Mini-UZI) 5.9lb (2.7kg). **Cartridge:** 9mm x 19 Parabellum or (UZI only) 0.45in Colt. **Feed:** (UZI) 25/32/40 box (9mm) or 16 box (0.45in); (Mini-UZI) 20/25/32 box (9mm only). **Rifling:** (9mm models) 4 groove r/h; (0.45in) 6 groove l/h. **Muzzle velocity:** (UZI) 1,312f/s (400m/s); (Mini-UZI) 1,148f/s (350m/s). **Effective range:** (UZI) 219yd (200m); (Mini-UZI) 164yd (150m). **Rate of fire:** (UZI) 600rpm; (Mini-UZI) 950rpm; (Micro-UZI) 1,200rpm.

At the end of the 1948 War Israel needed a reliable weapon which could be made from national resources in sufficient numbers to arm the bulk of the armed forces. A young Army major, Uziel Gal, designed just such a weapon, the UZI SMG, which is now one of the most widely used in the Western world.

He based his design on the pre-war Czechoslovak 9mm Models 23 and 25 SMGs. These had been designed to achieve greater accuracy than previous SMGs which were notoriously inaccurate. In these the bolt actually telescoped the rear end of the barrel, enclosing the cartridge, and the magazine was inserted through the pistol-grip so that the bolt face was at the point-of-balance and just forward of the shoulder axis, thus making the weapon more accurate when fired from the hip.

The UZI is a simple blow-back design. The bolt is cocked by drawing it to the rear and the sear rotates upwards to engage and hold it open. The simple trigger mechanism uses a coil spring to tension the sear; pulling the trigger allows the sear to move down and rotate out of engagement with the bolt. The bolt's own coil spring drives it forward, stripping a cartridge from the magazine, chambering it and firing it as the striker in the bolt face impacts the primer. The exploding cartridge then drives the bolt to the rear, extracting and ejecting the empty case, until it hits the bolt stop, where the spring drives it forward again to repeat the cycle.

The UZI is used in the armed forces of Belgium, the Federal Republic of Germany, Iran, the Netherlands, Thailand, Venezuela and other countries.

A smaller version — the Mini-UZI — differs mainly in size and weight, being small enough to conceal beneath ordinary clothing, making it especially suitable for certain special forces operations. It is available in open bolt, closed bolt and heavy bolt versions, the latter offering a reduced rate of fire (750rpm) to achieve better control.

Latest version is the Micro-UZI, just 10in (254mm) long, which makes it a large automatic pistol rather than a small SMG.

Above: 9mm Micro-UZI is the smallest, lightest version of the UZI family weighing just 4.7lb (2.14kg) fully loaded with 20 rounds. It is useful in maximum concealment situations.

Above: The Israeli 9mm UZI SMG is a blow-back weapon, in which the round is fired while the bolt is still travelling forward.

9mm L34A1 Sterling silenced sub-machine gun

Origin: United Kingdom. **Type:** Sub-machine gun. **Dimensions:** Stock extended 34.6in (864mm); stock folded 26.4in (660mm); barrel 7.9in (198mm). **Weights:** 8lb (3.6kg); loaded 9.5lb (4.3kg). **Caliber:** 9mm x 19 Parabellum. **Feed:** 34-round box magazine. **Rifling:** 6 grooves r/h. **Muzzle velocity:** Approximately 984f/s (300m/s). **Rate of fire:** (cyclic) 550rpm.

This is the silenced version of the L2A3, and is called the L34A1. It is somewhat longer than the L2A3 and tops the latter version's weight, unloaded, by almost two pounds (1kg). Many of its parts are interchangeable with those of the L2A3, thus keeping down replacement costs and ensuring weapon availability.

The barrel jacket is covered by a silencer casing, with front and rear supports. The barrel has 72 radial holes drilled through it, which permits propellant gas to escape, thus reducing the muzzle velocity of the bullet. The barrel has a metal wrap and diffuser tube; the extension tube goes beyond the silencer casing and barrel.

A spiral diffuser beyond the barrel is a series of discs, which has a hole through its center that allows passage of the round. Gas follows the round closely and is deflected back by the end cap; it mingles with the gases coming forward — with the result that the gas velocity leaving the weapon is low.

The silenced Sterling is used by the British Army, by many other countries, and terrorist groups. It is unusual among silenced SMGs in that it uses standard 9mm x 19 Parabellum rounds; other silent SMGs require special subsonic ammunition.

Right: British 'para' with an L34A1 fitted with a 10-round magazine. The L34A1 uses standard 9mm ammunition.

Below: Cutaway of the Sterling L34A1 shows radial holes in the barrel, the diffuser tube around the barrel and the spiral diffuser.

9mm Ingram Models 10/11

Origin: United States. **Type:** Sub-machine gun. **Dimensions:** Length (no stock), Model 10 10.5in (267mm), Model 11 8.7in (222mm); (telescoped) Model 10 10.6in (269mm); Model 11 9.8in (248mm); (extended) Model 10 21.6in (548mm), Model 11, 18.1in (460mm). Barrel, Model 10 5.75in (146mm), Model 11 5.1in (129mm). Suppressor, Model 10 11.5in (291mm), Model 11 8.8in (224mm). **Cartridge:** Model 10, 45 ACP; Model 11, 9mm Short (.380 ACP) or 9mm x 19 Parabellum. **Muzzle velocity:** Model 10, 924f/s (280m/s); Model 11, 967f/s (293m/s). **Rate of fire:** (cyclic) Model 10, 1,100rpm; Model 11, 1,200rpm.

This weapon is named after its inventor, Gordon B. Ingram, a practical man with clear views of what a good sub-machine gun should be. He designed a series of them after having fought in World War II, and all his weapons were simple, reliable, and relatively cheap to make.

In 1946 he produced his first version (the M5), but it was not the best of times to try and sell a new sub-machine gun since the world was full of surplus weapons. Undaunted, Ingram worked on a new model for two years and in 1949 set up a firm known as the Police Ordnance Company in partnership with some fellow veterans. The result was Model 6, which came in two types: one

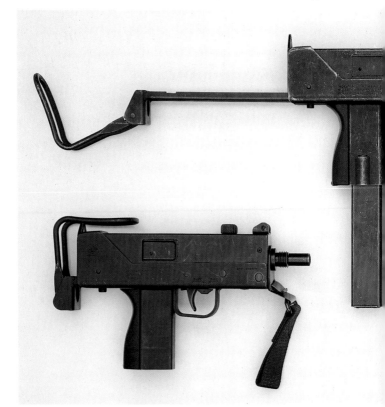

in .38in caliber, which looked like a Thompson, and another in .45in caliber, both of which sold well to police departments and in South America.

By 1959, Ingram had produced his Models 7 through 9, all of which were sufficiently successful to encourage him to go on with the series. In 1969, he went to work for a firm specializing in suppressors and during the next year this firm spun off a subsidiary. Now established, he began to design weapons which were entirely different from the earlier versions — and Models 10 and 11 soon appeared.

They are virtually identical except for size. Their overall appearance is similar in a general way to the early Webley automatic pistols; they work on blow-back, but have wraparound bolts which make it possible to keep the weapon short and improve control at full automatic fire. The cocking handle, which is on the top, is equally convenient for right- or left-handed firers; it has a slot cut in the center so as not to interfere with the line of sight. The magazine fits into the pistol-grip and the gun has a retractable butt.

The whole thing is made of stampings, with the exception of the barrel, and even the bolt is made of sheet metal and filled with lead. Models 10 and 11 are both fitted with suppressors, which reduce sound considerably. The modern-pattern Ingram — out of production for a while, but just recently returned to manufacture — is the primary standard arm of Portugal, Saudi Arabia and US special units. It has been sold to six other nations as well. Its chief virtue is power (to .45 ACP if desired) in a concealable package.

Below: Ingram silenced Model 10 (above) with component parts (below). Its great compactness makes it popular with special forces.

5.45mm AKR

Origin: Soviet Union.**Type:** Sub-machine gun.**Caliber:** 5.45mm.
Ammunition: 5.45 x 39.5 Soviet.**Dimensions:** Length (extended stock)
26.6in (675mm); (folded stock)16.5in (420mm).**Weight:** Not known.
Magazine: 30-round box type.**Muzzle velocity:** 2,625f/s (800m/s)(approx).
Effective range: 218yd (200m).**Rate of fire:** (cyclic) 800rpm (approx).

The Soviet Army used the 7.62mm PPSh-41 and PPS-43, fielded in 1941 and
1943 respectively, as its standard SMGs for many years. It then seemed to
allow the SMG as a type to die out, using AK-47 or AK-74 assault rifles where
other armies used SMGs. Recently, however, a totally new Soviet SMG has
appeared, which is clearly designed by Kalashnikov. The weapon is based
upon the AKS-74 assault rifle, but is much smaller and lighter.
    The barrel is very short (200mm) and is fitted with a screw-on, cylindrical
attachment at the front of which is a bell-shaped flash hider. Unlike the great
majority of SMGs the AKR fires standard, full-charge rifle ammunition (in this

case, Soviet 5.45 x 39.5). In addition, due to the shortness of the barrel the gas is tapped-off very close to the chamber and these two combine to create very high pressures in such a small weapon. The muzzle attachment appears, therefore, to be an expansion chamber intended to reduce the pressure acting on the gas piston and also to act as a flame damper.

Basic iron sights are fitted. The rear sight is a simple, flip-over device, which is marked for 219yd (200m) and 438yd (400m). Despite the use of rifle ammunition the latter marking seems somewhat optimistic and a maximum effective range of 218yd (200m) seems a reasonable assumption.

The internal mechanism is identical to that of the AK-47, except that the gas piston, return spring and spring guide rod are shorter. The weapon also has a very simple skeleton stock, which folds forwards along the left-hand side.

The AKR will undoubtedly be used by Soviet and other Warsaw Pact special forces units. It will also presumably be exported to Third World countries and Soviet client states in due course.

Below: 5.45mm AKR, the latest Soviet SMG, is based on the AKS-74, but is much smaller. Length with stock folded to the left (inset) and locked into a spring-loaded lug on the receiver is 16.5in (420mm).

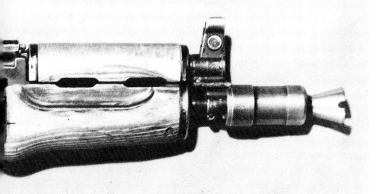

5.56mm SR88

Origin: Singapore. **Type:** Assault rifle. **Caliber:** 5.56mm. **Ammunition:** US M193 and M196. **Dimensions:** Length (less butt-stock) 29.37in (746mm). **Weight:** (unloaded) 8.07lb (3.66kg). **Magazine:** 20- or 30-round box type. **Muzzle velocity:** 3,182f/s (970m/s). **Effective range:** 437yd (400m). **Rate of fire:** (cyclic) 650-850rpm.

Above: Singapore's SR88, one of a number of 5.56mm rifle designs available, has done exceptionally well in trials around the world.

A number of increasingly sophisticated and complicated assault rifles have appeared over the past few years as designers have sought to include more features and increase 'capability'. Unfortunately, they seem to have forgotten that what any infantryman wants, whether he is a conventional soldier in an APC or a special forces man in a jungle ambush, is a thoroughly reliable, simple and accurate weapon, which continues to function even when dirty and regardless of having been dropped or whether the weather is very hot or very cold. What army budget holders want, since rifles are bought in huge quantities, is a weapon which is cheap to manufacture, has minimum maintenance requirements and which fires easy-to-obtain internationally standardised ammunition.

Like a number of other countries, the bustling Republic of Singapore entered the arms business by undertaking licence production in the 1960s of the US 5.56mm M16 Armalite rifle. A factory was established for the purpose by Chartered Industries of Singapore (CIS) and the rifle was used by the republic's armed forces in considerable numbers. CIS then designed and produced an excellent light machine gun, the 5.56mm Ultimax 100, which, with an empty weight (with bipod) of 10.47lb (4.7kg) is the lightest 5.56mm LMG on the market.

In the early 1970s the Singapore Army asked the firm to develop a more cost-effective rifle, which had to be simple, rugged, reliable, be economical to produce, using the most modern methods, and to be at least as good a weapon as the M16. Lacking its own in-house design capability, CIS selected Sterling Armament in the UK as designers; prototypes were constructed in 1978 and following troop trials, the SAR80 was put into full production in 1980.

The latest weapon is the new generation SR88, also a 5.56mm assault rifle, which is being adopted by several special forces in various countries around the world. This is a thoroughly sensible assault rifle. Conventional in design, it breaks no new technological ground but fully meets the criteria laid down for a rugged, reliable and easy-to-use assault weapon. SR88 is built on the straight line principle, with barrel, bolt recoil mechanism and stock all in line, dispersing firing impact into the shoulder, minimising barrel climb and increasing controllability and accuracy. It has four main assemblies.

The upper receiver assembly comprises the barrel, carrying handle and upper receiver. The barrel is fitted with a flash suppressor which vents sideways and upwards, and is made of high-grade steel with a chrome-plated chamber. The barrel connects to the receiver by a locknut and detent, simplifying barrel changes. The carrying handle is located between the barrel and receiver and is at the weapon's center of gravity. The second assembly — the gas piston — consists of a four-position, chrome-plated steel regulator, a piston-cum-push-rod and a return spring.

The bolt group assembly comprises the bolt carrier, bolt, buffer springs and rods. The bolt has seven lugs and rotates through 22.5° before locking. SR88 uses closed-bolt operation and can be fired in either the automatic or semi-automatic modes. A spring-loaded firing-pin prevents accidental discharge if the rifle is jolted or dropped. Finally, there is a stock and lower receiver assembly. The receiver is an aluminium forging which houses the firing mechanisms. The stock, made of glass fiber-reinforced nylon, is adjustable in length by adding or removing butt pads.

A very simple, but rugged and detachable bipod is available. Magazines are those used for the US M16, holding either 20 or 30 rounds. Other features include luminous sights, mountings for a scope, three-position firing control including a burst limiter, provision for a grenade launcher and an automatic lock on the cocking handle.

Below: SR88 removable butt version (top) and carbine (below). A well-designed weapon, it is proving popular with special forces.

5.56mm FA MAS rifle

Origin: France. **Type:** Assault rifle. **Dimensions:** Without bayonet 30.28in (757mm); barrel 19.51in (488mm). **Weights:** Without magazine, sling or bipod 7.94lb (3.61kg); magazine, .33lb (0.15kg) empty; .99lb (0.45kg) loaded with 25 rounds; bipod, .374lb (0.17kg). **Cartridge:** 5.56mm x 45 NATO: M193. **Effective range:** 330yd (300m). **Muzzle velocity:** 3,168f/s (960m/s). **Rate of fire:** (cyclic) 900-1,000rpm.

The FA MAS (Fusil Automatique, Manufacture d'Armes de St. Etienne) is France's newest service rifle and has proven to be a highly effective and generally well-conceived piece of ordnance for general service and special

forces use. First introduced in 1973 (and subsequently modified), the rifle was placed into production in 1979. Delivery of the first complement of 148,000 rifles was completed in 1983.

Firing from the closed-bolt position, the method of operation is by means of delayed blow-back, the system having been adopted from the French AA52 general purpose machine gun. A black plastic lower handguard, pinned to the barrel and receiver, extends to the magazine well and cannot be removed.

Because it has a "bullpup" configuration, the trigger mechanism and pistol-grip have been mounted to the lower handguard, forward of the magazine well. The pistol-grip is ergonomically designed, with three finger grooves and a

Below: One of the most compact of the new generation of 5.56mm assault rifles, the MAS is now in wide-scale use with the French including special force units such as the Foreign Legion.

storage trap that contains a bottle of lubricant. The sheet metal trigger guard can be pulled away from the rear retaining pin and rotated for firing with gloves under arctic conditions, an obvious advantage to mountain forces. The trigger is connected to a long, thin strip of sheet metal which rides in a slot on the right side of the receiver and reaches the hammer mechanism.

To remove a magazine, a spring-loaded plastic catch must be pressed back. Magazines are inserted by pushing them straight into the well.

Among the interesting features of the FA MAS are optional right- or left-side ejection and three-round burst mode as an alternative to single shot or fully automatic. With its high cyclic rate (900-1,000rpm), the three-shot burst mode is a real boon in controlling the weapon. Each weapon is equipped with an ambidextrous web sling. The foresight is mounted on a column pinned to the barrel; the rearsight is also on a column, above the return spring cylinder.

Versions of the FA MAS have scopes integrated into the carrying handles, as are short-barreled models with 16.5in (405mm) barrels. A new carrying handle that will accept any NATO STANAG scope is under development. The weapon is widely used among special troops such as France's naval infantry, Foreign Legion and paratroops.

A short version — the FA MAS Commando — is another variation available and is intended for use by commando and similar special forces. The barrel has been shortened to 16.2in (405mm), but in other respects is the same as the service weapon.

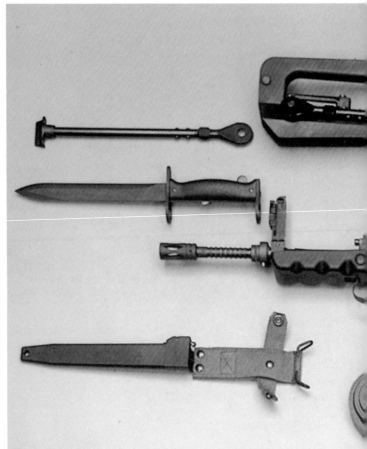

Above: French soldier firing the MAS. The butt brings recoil forces straight into the shoulder; built-in bipod helps accurate shooting.

Below: Components of the MAS illustrate simple, straightforward design. Bullpup design results in short, handy, easy-to-use weapon.

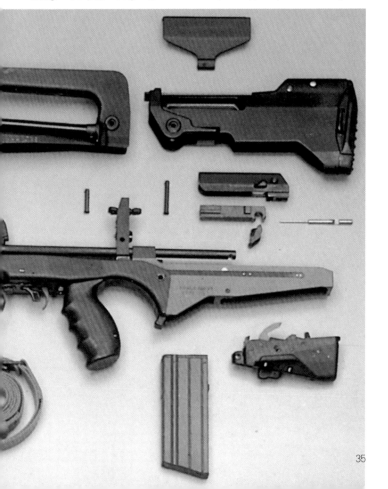

5.56mm & 7.62mm Galil assault rifle

Origin: Israel. **Type:** Assault rifle. **Dimensions:** Length, stock extended, 5.56 model 38.6in (979mm), 7.62 model 41.3in (1,050mm); stock folded, 5.56 model 29.2in (742mm), 7.62 model 31.9in (810mm). Barrel, 5.56 model 18.1in (460mm), 7.62 model 21 in (533mm). **Weight:** 5.56 model 8.6lb (3.9kg); 7.62 model 8.7lb (3.95kg). **Caliber:** 5.56mm or 7.62mm. **Max effective range:** 5.56 model 550yd (500m); 7.62 model 660yd (600m). **Muzzle velocity:** 5.56 model 3,230f/s (980m/s); 7.62 model 2,800f/s (850m/s). **Rate of fire:** Both models 650rpm.

Israel's Galil assault rifle, first issued in 1973, has a rich, battle-tested heritage. The system of the Galil is actually that of the Soviet AK-47 Kalashnikov, the most widely distributed and used of all assault rifles.

Credit for the rifle's development is given to an Israeli ordnance officer named Uziel Gal, along with Israel Military Industries. They realised that by using the full-scale Finnish Valmet M-60/62 receiver and a stout but not-too-heavy barrel, the system would serve both the 5.56 NATO cartridge and the 7.62 NATO round as well.

The operating system is a rotating bolt gas system and, with the exception of the stamped steel breech cover, the Galil is fully machined. The foregrip is wood, lined with Dural, and has ample clearance around the barrel for heat dissipation. When extended, the butt-stock has a positive latching system which prevents wobble by wedging the hinge end's tapered latching lugs into corresponding slots.

These are released by the simple expedient of squeezing with the right hand and folding the stock outward. The bipod folds and rotates into a slot on the underside of the foregrip, where the legs then spread apart by spring tension to latch into retaining slots.

The ambidextrous safety switch on the left side is a small lever, but its reciprocal right-side member also acts as an ejection port cover. The magazine is held by a catch in front of the trigger guard. To operate, the lever is taken off "safe" and the cocking handle pulled to the rear. When released, the carrier is driven forward and the top round is pushed from the magazine into the chamber.

The bolt comes to a halt and the cam pin (engaged in a slot in the carrier) rotates the bolt, which forces the cartridge forward, whereupon the extractor slips over the rim and the gun is ready to be fired.

Above: Israeli soldier with stock folded on his 5.56mm ARM assault rifle. The Galil has been thoroughly combat tested in many wars.

The system used for the trigger and firing mechanism is that employed in the M1 Garand rifle, the AK series and many others. Thirty-five rounds are held in the 5.56mm magazine and a 50-round magazine has also been produced. The 7.62mm magazine holds 25 rounds.

Sights for the Galil are folding "L" rear with two peeps, one for 330yd (300m), and a second for 550yd (500m). Unique to the system is its set of folding night sights which use tritium for illumination. For close quarter work at night or in a dark jungle, these sights are undetectable.

The Galil was adopted by South Africa after incorporating certain preferred modifications (such as carbon plastic stock instead of steel tubing to better fit terrain needs) and is called the R4 (Rifle 4). The R4 has proved itself in South West Africa and Angolan operations.

Below: Solid stock version of the very effective Galil 5.56mm automatic rifle, produced by Israel Military Industries (IMI).

5.56mm AR 70/223 Beretta

Origin: Italy. **Type:** Rifle. **Dimensions:** Length (overall), AR 70 39.8in (995mm), SC 70 38.4in (960mm); (butt folded), SC 70 29.4in (736mm); barrel, AR 70 18.0in (450mm), SC 70 18.0in (450mm). **Weights:** Empty, AR 70 8.4lb (3.8kg), SC 70 8.1lb (3.7kg); full magazine, AR 70 9.1lb (4.15kg), SC 70 9.2lb (4.2kg). **Cartridge:** 5.56mm x 45 NATO M193. **Rifling:** 4 grooves r/h, 1 turn in 12.2in (304mm). **Feed:** 30-round magazine. **Grenade:** 40mm. **Muzzle velocity:** 3,135f/s (950m/s). **Rate of fire:** (cyclic) 650rpm.

Beretta started work in 1968 to replace their 7.62mm BM 59 rifle, in service with the Italian Army, with an updated product. The project for a replacement was directed from the beginning by Vitorio Valle, head of the research and development department and P C Beretta, the company's general manager.

They evaluated the Stoner 63, M16A1, FN CAL and the Kalashnikov AK-47, hoping to come up with a blend of the best features, which they could then combine with their own innovations. The basic design was put in final form by 1970 — giving the weapon its name, Beretta Model 70.

The 70-series weapons fire from the closed-bolt position and are gas operated; there is no gas regulator. Since the gas port has been placed close to the muzzle end of the barrel, the system needs a 14in (355mm) piston. With the gas system located in the conventional position above the barrel, the magazine must feed from the bottom; however, balance and handling are enhanced by this location.

The trigger system is simple and clean. Semi-automatic fire is obtained by the usual disconnector between the trigger and sear. Upper and lower receiver bodies are sheet metal stampings, and guide rails and ejector are welded and riveted to the upper receiver shell. The hold-open system which retains the bolt group in the rearward position after the magazine has been emptied is almost identical to the one used on the M16.

There are two easily interchangeable butt-stock configurations. A high-impact rigid plastic stock with a steel butt plate is used on the assault rifle (AR 70) model. The butt-stock in the folding stock version (the SC 70 or Special Troops Carbine) is fabricated from tubular steel with an aluminium butt plate and plastic sleeve over the top tube.

In addition to Italian special forces, special forces of South Africa use the AR 70.

Below: Beretta AR 70, a traditional layout for a rifle, makes an interesting comparison with the revolutionary MAS (page 32).

Above: Italian soldier with Beretta Model 70. A folding-butt version of the rifle and a short carbine are also available.

5.45mm AK-74 and AKS-74

Origin: Soviet Union. **Type:** Assault rifles. **Dimensions:** Length (AK-74) 37in (930mm); (AKS-74, with butt folded) 28in (690mm); barrel 16in (40mm). **Weight:** (unloaded) (AK-74/AKS-74) 7.9lb (3.6kg). **Rifling:** 4 grooves r/h; 1 turn in 7.8in (196mm). **Cartridge:** 5.45mm x 39.5. **Feed:** 30-round plastic box magazine. **Effective range:** 495yd (450m). **Muzzle velocity:** 2,970f/s (900m/s). **Rate of fire:** (cyclic) 650rpm.

As indicated by its designation, the AK-74 assault rifle was developed in 1974 and probably entered service around 1977. The folding stock AKS-74, sometimes referred to as the AKD, was first seen with Soviet airborne troops in the Red Square Parade in Moscow on November 7, 1977.

The AK-74 is basically an AKM rechambered and rebored to fire a 5.45mm cartridge. Externally, it has the same general appearance as the AKM, with two notable differences: the AK-74 has a distinctive, two-port muzzle brake (giving it a slightly greater overall length than the AKM), and a smooth plastic magazine which is slightly shorter and is curved to a lesser extent than the grooved metal AKM. It uses the same type bayonet as the AK series weapons. The folding stock version, designated AKS-74, has a Y-shaped tubular stock with an extremely narrow butt-plate, as opposed to the T-shaped, stamped-metal butt-stock of the AKMS.

The muzzle brake on the AK-74 uses a fluidic device to minimise recoil and muzzle climb. Although the AK-74 is somewhat heavier than the AKM when empty, its loaded weight is slightly less, primarily because of the plastic magazine and its smaller caliber ammunition, which can inflict a particularly nasty wound. There are reports the AKS now has a Soviet version of the US M203 grenade launcher.

Above: Soviet Army paratroopers on parade with their AKS-74, folding-stock version of the Kalashnikov AK-74 assault rifle.

Among the limitations of the rifle are that the gas cylinder is in a vulnerable position and, if dented, may cause weapon malfunction, and that the reddish-brown or orange colour of the plastic magazine does not lend itself to camouflage.

Above: AK-74 assault rifle with folded stock. Cutaway areas reveal the ammunition and piston mechanisms.

7.62mm AK-47 and AKM

Origin: Soviet Union. **Type:** Assault rifle. **Dimensions:** (AK-47): butt extended 34.8in (869mm); butt folded 30in (699mm); barrel 16.6in (414mm); (AKM): length 35in (876mm); barrel 16.6in (414mm). **Weights:** (AK-47) 9.5lb (4.3kg); (AKM) 6.9lb (3.15kg). **Cartridge:** 7.62mm x 39 M 1943. **Feed:** 30-round detachable box magazine. **Effective range:** 330yd (300m). **Muzzle velocity:** (AK-47) 2,343f/s (710m/s); (AKM) 2,360f/s (715m/s). **Rate of fire:** (cyclic) 600rpm.

The Soviet Army has always understood the value of sheer volume of fire, particularly if it could be produced by not very highly trained troops firing simple weapons. During World War II, they had seen and been impressed by the German MP44. When the war was over, they set out — with the assistance of German designers — to produce a similar weapon.

This led to the Avtomat-Kalashnikova assault rifle. Although designed in 1947 and thus referred to as the AK-47, the AK was actually adopted in 1949 and entered service in 1951. The AK was the basic infantry weapon of the Soviet Army until the introduction of the AKM, which was developed in 1959 and entered service in 1961. All 7.62 Kalashnikov assault weapons are highly dependable weapons. They produce a high volume of fire and are simple to maintain. The AK-47 is accurate and sufficiently heavy to shoot well in automatic at the ranges likely to be required in modern war — up to 330yd (300m) — without undue vibration.

Produced in greater quantity than any other modern small arm, the AK-47 and AKM can fairly be said to have set a new standard in infantry weapons. The original AK-47 came with a wooden stock or (for AFV crews,

Below: Soviet 7.62mm assault rifles: Simonov (top), AKMS (center), standard AK-47 (bottom), plus AKM bayonet and Makarov PM pistol.

paratroopers and motorcyclists) a folding metal stock. It uses a short cartridge firing a stubby bullet. A gas-operated weapon with rotating bolt (which is often chrome-plated), it can readily be used by troops all over the world, of any standard of education, and gives extremely reliable results under the most adverse conditions. Versions with various designations have been produced in at least five countries, and it is used in at least 35 armies.

The curved magazine and silhouette are hallmarks of terrorists and guerrillas in Lebanon, Syria, South Yemen, Mozambique, Angola, Zimbabwe and Central America.

The present standard Soviet infantry small arm is the AKM, an amazingly light weapon that makes extensive use of metal stampings and plastic, and has a cyclic-rate reducer, compensator and other improvements. Both rifles can be fitted with luminous sights or the NSP-2 infra-red sight and a bayonet, which doubles as a saw and an insulated wire cutter.

Below: Special forces learn to use foreign weapons: US Special Forces soldier holds a Type 56 rifle, Chinese version of the AK-47.

5.56mm Colt Commando

Origin: United States. **Type:** Assault rifle/sub-machine gun. **Dimensions:** Length (butt extended) 31.5in (787mm), (butt telescoped) 28.4in (711mm); barrel 10.2in (254mm). **Weight:** (with sling and loaded) 7.1lb (3.23kg). **Cartridge:** 5.56mm x 45 NATO M193. **Feed:** 20- and 30-round box magazine. **Rifling:** 4 groove r/h. **Effective range:** 219yd (200m). **Muzzle velocity:** 3,049f/s (924m/s). **Rate of fire:** (cyclic) 700-800rpm.

The Colt Commando is essentially a shorter and handier version of the AR-15 and was developed for use in Vietnam for battle at close quarters. Mechanically, it is identical to the AR-15, but with a much shorter barrel than the 21in (533mm) barrel of the rifle. This reduces the muzzle velocity slightly and has a serious effect on accuracy at longer ranges; it also causes considerable muzzle flash, which made it necessary to incorporate a 4in (100mm) flash hider which can be unscrewed if necessary.

The Colt Commando has a telescopic butt which can be pulled out when it is required to fire from the shoulder, and in spite of the limitations on accuracy imposed by the shorter barrel, the weapon proved useful in Vietnam. It features selective fire and a holding-open device and is actuated by the same direct gas action.

Designed as a survival weapon, it filled the sub-machine gun role so well that it was issued to US Special Operations Forces. It is also believed to be in limited use by the British SAS.

Below: 5.56mm Colt Commando is essentially a shortened version of the M16 for use by special forces in close-quarter battle.

Above: Colt Commando has a short barrel with considerable muzzle flash; hence the rather large, 4in (100mm) long flash hider.

5.56mm M16A1/A2

Origin: United States. **Type:** Assault rifle. **Dimensions:** Length overall (with flash suppressor) 38.9in (990mm); M16A2 40.0in (1,000mm); barrel 19.8in (508mm). **Weights:** M16A1 7.0lb (3.18kg); M16A2 7.5lb (3.4kg); with standard 30-round magazine 8.2lb (3.72kg); sling 5.3oz (182g). **Caliber:** 5.56mm x 45 M193. **Feed:** 20- and 30-round box magazine. **Maximum effective range:** M16A1 300yd (274m); M16A2 875yd (800m). **Muzzle velocity:** 3,280f/s (1,000m/s). **Rate of fire:** 700-950rpm (cyclic); 150-200rpm (auto); 45-65rpm (semi-automatic).

The M16 (previously the AR-15), designed by Eugene Stoner, was a development of the earlier 7.62mm AR-10 assault rifle. It was adopted for use in Vietnam and when first used in combat, numerous faults became apparent, most of them traceable to a lack of training and poor maintenance. Since then the M16A1 has replaced the 7.62mm M14 as the standard rifle of the United States forces.

Millions have been manufactured, most by Colt Firearms. The weapon was also made under license in Singapore, the Republic of Korea and the Philippines. Twenty-one armies currently use the M16.

The weapon is gas-operated and the user can select either full-automatic or semi-automatic. Both 20- and 30-round magazines can be fitted, as can a bipod, bayonet, telescope and night sight. The weapon can also be fitted with the M203 40mm grenade launcher, and this fires a variety of 40mm grenades to a maximum range of 382yd (350m). The M203 has now replaced the M79 grenade launcher.

The Commando sub-machine gun model of the M16 is a special version with a shorter barrel, flash suppressor and a telescopic sight, reducing the overall length of the weapon to 27.9in (710mm). It is in use with US Special Operations Forces. The M231 is a special model which can be fired from within the M2 Bradley Infantry Fighting Vehicle.

There has been consistent dissatisfaction with the M16A1 in the US Army, and even more so in the other main user — the US Marine Corps. One of the major complaints is its lack of effectiveness at ranges above 340yd (300m), which has come to a head with the increased emphasis on desert warfare. This, combined with the high average age of current stocks, led to a major review in 1981. The result, the M16A2, is a rifle that is actually a throwback to the 1950s; it is a weapon that has finally come full circle to where it should have begun in the first place. It entered inventories in 1987.

The barrel of the M16A2 is heavier, with a thicker profile. It weighs 8.15lb (3.69kg) with sling and empty 30-round magazine compared to the 7.9lb (3.58kg) of the M16A1. Other major changes include a three-round burst

Above: M16A1 is one of the most widely used rifles in the world; here with a New Zealand SAS soldier on jungle exercise in Fiji.

device, intended to cut down ammunition waste from the full-automatic operation on the A1; a new rearsight with a windage knob; a square-edged front sight post to give better target definition; a butt-stock and handguard made of stronger materials; a flash suppressor that doubles as a muzzle compensator; and a wedge-shaped projection at the rear of the ejection port to deflect hot brass away from the face of the left-handed shooter.

Most importantly, the requirements for a longer-range weapon have been met by rebarreling to use the new NATO 5.56mm round more effectively. The longer, heavier bullets of these rounds are fully stabilised by the M16A2's barrel, which is rifled with a twist of one turn in seven inches (one in 177mm). This improves the maximum effective range to about 875yd (800m).

Below: The classic assault rifle of the 1960s and 1970s, the M16A1 was designed by Eugene Stoner; millions have been manufactured.

7.62mm Accuracy International Model PM

Origin: United Kingdom. **Type:** Sniper rifle. **Caliber:** 7.62mm x 51 NATO.
Dimensions: Length (extended) 47in (1,194mm). **Weight:** 14.3lb (6.5kg).
Magazine: 10-round box type. **Effective range:** 1,094yd (1,000m).

In the 1960s and 1970s there was a move away from sniper rifles, which seemed to many people to have been overtaken by progress in modern warfare. The error of this assumption has now been recognised and many special units are now re-equipping with sniper rifles, either specialist adaptations of standard infantry weapons, or, as in the case of the British Army, with specially developed weapons like the Accuracy International 7.62mm PM sniper rifle system, officially designated L96A1. This weapon is now in service with the SAS and SBS, and is replacing the Lee Enfield 7.62mm L42A1 sniper rifle (a conversion of the Lee Enfield 0.303in Service rifle) in the infantry.

The principal criteria to which the PM was designed are: guaranteed first-shot accuracy, unchanging zero, a stock unaffected by environmental changes, a bipod, adjustable stock and trigger to suit individual users, telescopic sight, robustness, reliability, interchangeability and economy. The first of these was obviously the most important and a crucial factor identified by the design team during their research was that in conventional designs the accuracy falls off rapidly with weapon use due, to a large degree, to bedding surfaces opening up. The solution A.I. have selected is to use a massive and very stiff *integral chassis,* which is impervious to environmental changes and is precisely reproducible.

The barrel is made of stainless steel, giving excellent corrosion and erosion resistance, and a normal accuracy life in excess of 5,000 rounds. It attaches to the action by a screw thread bedding against a locking-ring, and can be changed in approximately 5 minutes without stripping the rifle. Such simplicity is a characteristic of the weapon and the sniper can carry out all but the most major repairs on his weapon himself, three Allen keys and a screwdriver being the only tools required to strip the rifle completely.

All accessories mate directly to the chassis, including the stock, butt spacers, sling swivels, trigger unit, magazine and catch, handstop and bipod. The stock does not form a structural part of the weapon and is carefully designed to be equally suitable for use by right- or left-handed firers. It is made

Right: A significant advance in sniper rifles, the PM is now in service with British SAS and SBS as well as infantry snipers.

Above: PM's integral chassis is impervious to environmental change.

of scuff-resistant, olive-drab, matt finish plastic and comes in two halves.

Testing showed that the greatest accuracy was obtained using a bipod (rather than a sling), with the firer's left hand under the stock, his right hand on the pistol-grip and the rifle pushed forward into the bipod. To further assist the sniper an optional spike is available, which fits into a retractable housing under the stock. This allows the sniper on a protracted operation to set his rifle on the target and then leave it while he rests or relaxes; he can then return without having to waste time searching for the target.

A universal rail is machined into the top of the action, upon which all types of sighting scopes, night-sight brackets and iron sights can be mounted. Accuracy International has worked with the West German firm of Schmidt und Bender to develop sights particularly suited to the PM system, although other types such as Pilkington Kite, Osprey OE 8050 and Simrad Optronics KN250 night sights can also be fitted. The Schmidt und Bender sights are of two types: 12 x 42 and 2.5-10 x 56, the latter having the highest light-gathering capability of any sight currently available, with the added advantage that varying the power does not affect the mean point-of-impact (MPI).

The PM comes in a variety of models, optimised for particular requirements. The standard version, PM Infantry, has a standard barrel, iron sights, 6 x 42 telescopic sight and a bipod. The Moderated Model PM uses a special barrel, while other versions are designed specifically for counter-terrorist and covert operations. A barrel fitted with a flash-eliminator is also available.

7.62mm Heckler & Koch PSG1

Origin: Federal Republic of Germany. **Type:** Sniper rifle. **Dimensions:** Length 46.7in (1,210mm); barrel 25.6in (650mm). **Weights:** Without magazine 17.85lb (8.1kg); magazine empty 9.88oz (276g). **Cartridge:** 7.62mm x 51 NATO. **Feed:** 5- or 20-round magazine.

A new member of the Group 1 series of Heckler & Koch rifles, the *Präzisionsschützengewehr* (High-precision Marksman's Rifle) PSG 1 has been developed for police and service sniper use. It is a semi-automatic, single-shot weapon using H&K's roller-locked bolt system.

The semi-automatic PSG1 is based on the G3 military assault rifle, which has been proven in service with 50 nations. It is fitted with a polygon-bored heavy barrel, and the trigger, fitted with an adjustable trigger shoe, is normally set to break at 3.3lb (1.49kg). A special low-noise bolt-closing device is fitted, and the stock has an adjustable comb and butt pad that allow fitting to individual shooters. A bipod attaches directly to the stock.

The PSG1 is topped with the state-of-the-art Hensoldt 6 x 42 scope with LED-enhanced manual reticle. The scope-mounted activator produces a helpful red dot for approximately 30 seconds, plenty of time to get off that critical shot. The scope mounts directly on the PSG1's permanent base.

Windage and elevation adjustment is by moving lens, six settings from 110 to 655yd (100 to 600m), and there is a fine adjustment facility to compensate for any mounting offset angle.

Right above: The PSG1 sniping rifle was developed for police and special forces. It uses the H&K roller-locked bolt system.

Right: Numerous adjustments are possible, including butt-stock length, pivotted butt cap and vertically movable cheek piece.

Below: Designed for the specialist and highly trained marksman, the PSG1 is one of the most effective sniper rifles available.

7.62mm G3SG/1 sniper rifle

Origin: Federal Republic of Germany. **Type:** Sniper rifle. **Dimensions:** Length, fixed butt 42.2in (1,025mm); retractable butt 33.6in (840mm); barrel 18.0in (450mm). **Weight:** Unloaded, with sight 12.2lb (5.54kg). **Cartridge:** 7.62mm x 51 NATO. **Feed:** 20-round box magazine. **Range:** 656yd (600m). **Rifling:** 4 grooves r/h, 1 turn in 12.2in (305mm). **Muzzle velocity:** 2,560-2,625f/s (780-800m/s). **Rate of fire:** (cyclic) 500-600rpm; (auto) 100rpm.

It was much of the work on assault rifles such as the Stg 45(M) during World War II that supplied the design information for the Heckler & Koch G3. After a development phase in Spain with the weapon (using an unusually long 7.92mm bullet), further development work was transferred to Heckler & Koch in Stuttgart. The G3 replaced the FN FAL rifle in the Bundeswehr in 1959.

Current models make extensive use of plastic and stampings; only the barrel and bolt components are machined. Designed for semi- and fully automatic fire, the weapon has a three-position selector/safety lever above the pistol-grip on the left side.

A standard feature of the rifle, which enhances accuracy, is the roller-delayed blow-back action, which requires no gas to be bled off, and no piston either. Since there are no fittings attached to the barrel, there is nothing to interfere with the barrel's harmonic variable.

Retaining the G3's iron sights, the SG/1 modification allows for the use of the same quick release scope mount that clamps to its parent. The glass in the mount is the Zeiss diavan 1.5-6x scope, which features excellent clarity and good light gathering.

The G3SG/1 uses a modified trigger which features a "set" lever behind the trigger itself, the use of which reduces the pull to 2.75lb (1.247kg). One other area in which the G3SG/1 is different from its parent is that the butt-stock is fitted with a detachable comb which allows for up to an inch (25.4mm) of

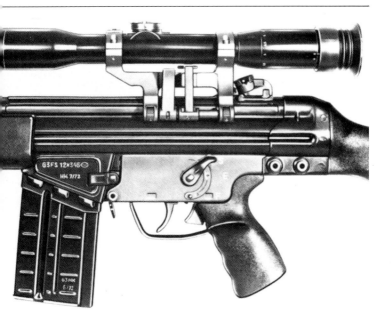

Above: G3SG/1 is used by the West German and other police forces as a sniper rifle; it has a Zeiss 1.5x to 6x telescopic sight.

variation for proper eye-to-scope orientation.

The G3 is in service with the armed forces of at least 12 countries; the G3SG/1 sniper rifle is in use with the Federal Republic of Germany's crack GSG 9 counter-terrorist unit, the Italian carabinieri, and other police forces.

Below: G3SG/1 sniper rifle is used by Federal Germany's GSG-9.

7.62mm Dragunov (SVD) sniper rifle

Origin: Soviet Union. **Type:** Sniper rifle. **Dimensions:** Length 48.2in (1,227mm). **Weight:** (with POS-1 sight) (empty) 9.4lb (4.3kg); (loaded) 10.5lb (4.78kg). **Cartridge:** 7.62mm x 54 rimmed. **Effective range:** 1,420yd (1,300m). **Muzzle velocity:** 2,725f/s (830m/s). **Rate of fire:** (semi-automatic) 30rpm.

The SVD was developed in 1965 and entered service in 1967. It is the standard Soviet sniper weapon. One squad in each motorised rifle platoon has an SVD, and selected riflemen receive regular, centralised sniper training. Largely due to its open butt-stock, the SVD is lighter than older sniper rifles.

Both the bolt mechanism and the gas recovery system are similar to those of the AK and AKM assault rifles; however, because of the difference in cartridges, parts of it are not interchangeable with these weapons. The most distinguishing features of the SVD are the open butt-stock, fitted with a cheek pad for easy sighting, and a telescopic sight over the receiver.

It has a combination flash suppressor/compensator and can mount the standard AKM bayonet. Four magazines, a cleaning kit, and an extra battery and lamp for the telescopic sight are issued with the weapon.

Even though it is equipped with a bayonet, the rifle is not an ideal weapon for close combat because it can fire only in the semi-automatic mode. Its weight and length also limit its manoeuvrability, but snipers work alone and take their time about moving, so this is not a serious problem.

The Soviet Army has always set great store by sniping and in World War II men were specially trained to spot German officers by their badges of rank and then shoot them.

Right: The telescopic sight used on the SVD is a detachable, non-variable, 4x scope, with an extension tube to give eye relief.

Below: The 7.62mm Dragunov (SVD) is now the standard sniper rifle for Soviet special forces; it is simple and very accurate.

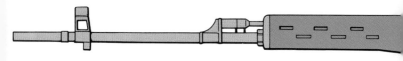

Above: The SVD incorporates the lessons learned by the Soviets over many years of concentrated effort in military sniping.

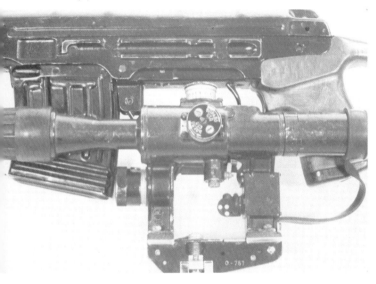

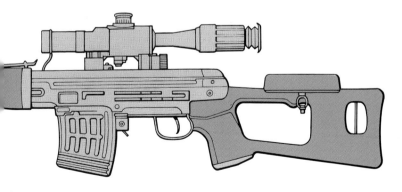

12-bore Franchi SPAS 12

Origin: Italy. **Type:** Anti-riot shotgun. **Dimensions:** Length 37.2in (930mm); (stock folded) 28.4in (710mm); barrel 18.4in (460mm). **Weight:** 9.2lb (4.2kg). **Caliber:** 12 bore. **Rate of fire:** 250rpm (theoretical); 24-30rpm (practical).

This Special Purpose Automatic Shotgun (SPAS) was first produced in October 1979 by the firm of Luigi Franchi Development. It was based on the perception that a specific riot shotgun was needed, that shotguns then in use were largely modified sport models, and that a military/police weapon in this area was the answer.

The gun itself has a skeleton butt and a special device enabling it to be fired with one hand if the occasion dictates. Short barreled and semi-automatic, the receiver is composed of light alloy and other parts (barrel and gas cylinder) are chromed to resist corrosion.

Automatic action of the shotgun permits it to fire about four shots a second. Using standard buckshot rounds, it can put 48 pellets a second on a target at almost 44yd (40m). It uses a wide range of ammunition: buck-shot, solid slug, small pellets and tear gas rounds. With a grenade launcher fitted to the muzzle, it can fire grenades out to a maximum range of nearly 165yd (150m). A special scattering device also fits on the muzzle and produces an instantaneous spread of pellets.

The Model 12 differs slightly from the Model 11, the main differences being in the fore-end and the improved and strengthened folding stock.

Above: Franchi Model 12 SPAS has a folding stock with a forearm rest enabling it to be fired with one hand, as shown here.

Below: SPAS Model 12 is a short-barreled semi-automatic shotgun of simple and reliable design; it can fire four rounds per second.

12-bore Ithaca 37

Origin: United States. **Type:** Police/military shotgun. **Dimensions:**
Length 18.8 to 20in (470-508mm). **Weights:** 6.5 to 7lb (2.94-3.06kg).
Caliber: 12-bore, 2¾in. **Feed:** 5- or 8-shot tubular magazine.

This shotgun is the famed basic "Featherlight" Model 37 pump action
repeater manufactured by the Ithaca Gun Company of Ithaca, New York. It is
a weapon that is uniquely free of stamped steel components, even to the trigger group.

The solid steel receiver does not have the usual ejection port on the right
because it pops empty shells straight out of the bottom. Its unique action is
centered around a dual-duty shell carrier that lifts live shells up to feed straight
into the chamber.

Its pistol-grip affords greater control while firing from the shoulder, and
makes it practical to fire from a hip position.

The type of barrel in Ithaca's "Deerslayer" model (a trade-mark of the company to indicate precision-bored cylindrical barrels for general hunting uses)
has been fitted to a combat shotgun. The objective is to provide a weapon
capable of firing rifle slugs with optimum accuracy as well as capable of handling the usual loadings. It is designated the 12-gauge DS Police Special.

A number of short-barrelled cylinder-bored configurations have been put in
use by military and police forces in the US.

12-bore Mossberg 500 ATP8

Origin: United States. **Type:** Police/military shotgun. **Dimensions:**
Length, ATP8 40.3in (1,009mm), ATP8C (pistol-grip) 30.9in (762mm);
barrel, ATP8 20.3in (308mm), ATP8C (pistol-grip) 20.3in (508mm).
Weights: ATP8 6.7lb (3.06kg), ATP8C (pistol-grip) 6.1lb (2.72kg). **Caliber:**
12-bore, 2¾ or 3in. **Magazine capacity:** 8-shot tubular.

The basic series of Mossberg 500 shotguns is specially modified for police and
military use. They have been described by some, as have other shotguns, as
"reloadable Claymores".

There are two main types — the six-shot and eight-shot models — but it is
the latter which is used by special forces. Its design is such as to ensure maximum reliability in use. It has an aluminium receiver for good balance and light
weight. A cylinder-bored barrel, which is proof-tested to full magnum loads,
provides optimum dispersion patterns and allows a variety of ammunition to
be fired.

The shotgun has twin extractors and the slide mechanism has twin guide
bars that help prevent twisting or jamming during rapid operation. A recent
addition is that the muzzle has been formed into a muzzle brake by cutting
slots in the upper surface. Gas can then be expelled in such a way as to exert
downward force, thus permitting easier pointing. In its pistol-grip form, the
Mossberg ATP8 is extremely compact and can thus be stowed more easily inside vehicles.

There is an almost infinite variety of options available. Latest model is the
Bullpup 12 shot-gun version of the Mossberg 500. This consists of the basic
Model 500 action inside a totally new framework made from impact-resistant
thermoplastic material.

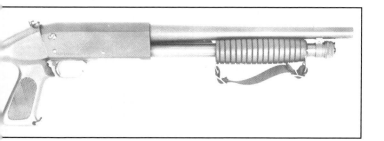

Above: The Ithaca Model 37 'Stakeout' is so compact (the barrel is just 13.3in (336mm) long) that it can be hidden under a topcoat.

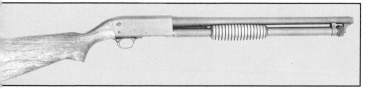

Above: Ithaca Model 37 M&P shotgun with long, 8-round magazine.

Above: The US Mossberg company makes a series of 12-gauge pump-action shotguns for police, military and sporting use.

37mm ARWEN 37

Origin: United Kingdom. **Type:** Anti-riot weapon. **Dimensions:** Adjustable length 29.9in (760mm) to 33.1in (840mm). **Weights:** 6.8lb (3.1kg) empty; 8.4lb (3.8kg) loaded. **Caliber:** 37mm. **Ammunition:** (Type AR1) baton, range 65 to 330ft (20-100m); (Type AR2) multi-source irritant smoke, range 280 to 310ft (85-95m); (Type AR3) baton with discrete dose of CS irritant, range 7 to 165ft (2-50m); (Type AR4) multi-source screening smoke, range 280 to 310ft (85-95m); (Type AR5): non-pyrotechnic barricade-penetrating irritant. **Rate of fire:** 60 rpm; sustained rate of 12 aimed shots/minute.

In 1977, the British Ministry of Defence drafted a requirement for a multi-shot weapon for use in Northern Ireland. By 1979, the Royal Small Arms Factory Enfield (now Royal Small Arms Limited) had produced three candidates. The first was a pump-action weapon with a four-shot capacity; the second was a revolver-action weapon with a five-shot capacity; and the third was a self-loading weapon, fitted with a box magazine. In addition to the weapons, a prototype baton round was also developed.

Following trials of the prototypes, it was decided in early 1981 that a final mockup development would be produced. This incorporated the barrel and revolving action of prototype two with the trigger/pistol-grip and stock of prototype three. There were other modifications and developments, but the resulting anti-riot weapon was designated the ARWEN 37. (Anti-Riot Weapon Enfield).

The caliber was selected because it is the optimum size for the required energy/velocity combination. It is equipped with a rifled twist of 1-in-21in (1-in-540mm) for optimum accuracy. The pistol-grip and trigger housing contain an integral ambidextrous safety lever. The weapon, as an additional safety feature, is fully cocked only when the first pressure is fully taken up. Upon release of the trigger, the action returns to the uncocked state.

The trigger is designed for operation by both index and middle fingers. Taking up the second pressure on the trigger and releasing it fires the weapon and revolves the feeding mechanism, bringing the next round into line with the breech. Recoil is not heavy. The revolving feed mechanism is easily removed for cleaning. The ARWEN 37 is loaded through the open port on the right side, and this loading aperture also acts as an ejection port for ejecting cartridges automatically.

Above: ARWEN Ace is a single-shot weapon designed for use by special forces and police, firing 37mm anti-riot munitions.

Its sights are currently of the folding aperture type, though it is planned to replace this with a single optical sight with integral reticule illumination.

The ARWEN 37V has been developed for use in armoured vehicles and is fitted with an optical sight on an extended stem. Its barrel is of a slightly different exterior configuration to the ARWEN 37, and it is not fitted with a stock.

In any of its different configurations, ARWEN provides police or paramilitary forces with a highly effective and flexible method for containing situations involving riots and civil disobedience.

A recent development is the ARWEN ACE, a single-shot device firing the same ammunition as the ARWEN 37, but without the 'political' sensitivities of an automatic weapon.

Below: ARWEN 37 is a multi-shot, self-loading, semi-automatic anti-riot weapon with a 5-round magazine of simple design.

70mm ARMSEL Striker

Origin: South Africa. **Type:** Police/military shotgun. **Gauge:** 12 gauge, 2¾in (70mm). **Dimensions:** Length: 20in (500mm) with butt folded; 31.2in (78cm) with stock extended. Barrel: 11.8in (300mm). **Weight:** 9.25lb (4.2kg) unloaded. **Practical range:** 165 to 120ft (50 to 70m). **Rate of fire:** 12 rounds/3s.

The "Striker" shotgun — second name "The Protector" — is the invention of a Rhodesian farmer, who developed it as a counter-terrorist weapon for use in the Rhodesian bushwar (1972-80).

At the conclusion of the Rhodesian bush campaign, the "Striker" found a home in South Africa and is now manufactured in Johannesburg as a potential military, security and anti-terrorist weapon. It does not conform to any standard shotgun configuration, its windup coil spring-driven 12-round drum magazine being actuated by a two-phase, double-action, trigger-indexing mechanism.

Because of its great controllability, it can be fired with one hand like a pistol with complete control for repeat shots. The "Striker's" balance sits between

the hands via twin pistol-grips, which are of fiberglass-reinforced poly-carbonate. The safety button is at the top of the rear pistol-grip just to the rear of the trigger, and runs from side to side at 90 degrees to the center line.

This safety is trigger locking, but a built-in feature prevents it from firing even if dropped. This is because the chambers of the magazine are out of alignment with the barrel and the firing-pin until the double-action trigger is pulled through its primary stage.

Its unchoked barrel has a practical range of 55 to just over 75yd (50 to 70m), but the "Striker" is also listed as dangerous when used with buckshot or slugs to just beyond 545yd (500m). Recoil and muzzle rise are relatively negligible in both one- and two-handed firing; the optional sight for the gun also aids in accuracy. The sight is a small (5.5in/140mm) and light (4.5oz/127g) day or night sight mounted like a telescope sight with windage and elevation adjustments.

It is now sold mainly as a home defence and police/security guard gun. According to accounts, while a number of mining concerns in South Africa have bought the "Striker" for security forces, some foreign military anti-terrorist units may be considering its purchase.

Below: The unusual ARMSEL Striker is an automatic, 12-bore shotgun with a clockwork 12-round magazine.

5.56mm M249 Squad Automatic Weapon (SAW)

Origin: Belgium. **Type:** General-purpose machine gun. **Dimensions:** (Standard model) overall 40.9in (1,040mm), barrel 18.4in (466mm); (Para model) overall (stock unfolded) 35.5in, (900mm), (stock folded) 28.5in (725mm), barrel 13.7in (347mm). **Weight:** (Standard model) 15.2lb (6.875kg); (Para model) 15lb (6.8kg). **Cartridge:** 5.56mm x 45 (FN SS109 (NATO) or M193 (US)). **Feed:** 100- or 200-round belts, or 30-round box magazine. **Rifling:** 6 grooves r/h; (SS109) 1 turn in 178mm, (M193) 1 turn in 304mm. **Muzzle velocity:** (SS109) 3,000f/s (915m/s); (M193) 3,166 f/s (965m/s). **Effective range:** 1,421yd (1,300m). **Rate of fire:** (cyclic) 750-1,000rpm.

The M249 SAW is a development of the Belgian Fabrique Nationale (FN) "Minimi" for the US Army. Original orders were met from the FN factory, but a production line has now been set up in the USA; current requirements are for 26,000 for the Army and 9,000 for the US Marine Corps, but many more may eventually enter service.

The US Army's Squad Automatic Weapon (SAW) idea was conceived in 1966, but has taken some time to reach service. When the 5.56mm M16 rifle was issued to infantry squads all men in the squad had an automatic weapon, but with a maximum effective range of little more than 330yd (300m). It was considered that both fire teams in the squad needed a weapon of greater all-round capability than the M16, but obviously not as heavy or sophisticated as the 7.62mm M60 LMG. The SAW meets this requirement and is being issued on a scale of one per fire team.

The M249 is very smooth in operation and displays an exceptional degree of reliability. Fully combat ready, with a magazine of 200 rounds, bipod, sling and cleaning kit, the M249 weighs just 22lb (9.97kg), which is still 1lb (0.4kg) less than an empty M60 LMG! The Minimi is most unusual in that it can accept either magazine- or belt-feed without any modification. The gun is normally

Above: US soldier fires a 5.56mm M249 Minimi SAW from the hip.

fired from the bipod, but a tripod is available. There is also a Para model, with a sliding stock and shorter barrel; it is little lighter than the standard version but is easier to handle in vehicles and helicopters.

The Minimi/M249 has already been ordered for the US, Canadian and Indonesian armed forces and can be expected to be found in many more in the next decade. Its small size, light weight and great reliability make it very suitable for special forces' use.

Below: In the US forces the M249 is replacing M16A1 rifles in the SAW role; it can be either belt- or magazine-fed.

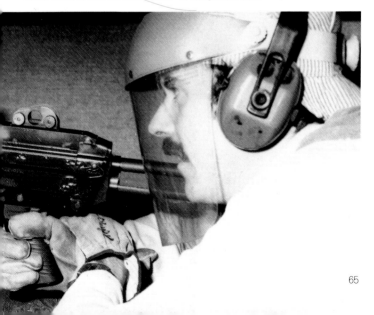

7.62mm L7A2 machine gun

Origin: United Kingdom. **Type:** General-purpose machine gun.
Dimensions: Length overall 49.3in (1,232mm); barrel (with flash
suppressor) 23.9in (597mm). **Weights:** With light barrel 23.9lb (10.9kg);
barrel 6.0lb (2.73kg). **Caliber:** 7.62mm x 51 NATO. **Feed:** Belt. **Effective
range:** On bipod 880yd (800m); on tripod 1,540yd (1,400m). **Muzzle
velocity:** 2,765f/s (838m/s). **Rate of fire:** (cyclic) 750-1,000rpm.

At the close of World War II, the British Army had the Vickers Mark I machine
gun as its sustained fire weapon and the Bren as its section light machine gun.
They both used a .303in rimmed cartridge.

Following introduction of the NATO 7.62mm round, the Bren was adapted
for the new round. Designated 7.62mm L4A1 this was a very successful and
popular weapon, still widely used around the world. However, the British Army decided that the opportunity was available to select a modernised general-
purpose machine gun. The Belgian *Mitrailleuse d'Appui Général* (MAG) was
chosen after many trials, and built under license at the Royal Small Arms Factory, Enfield as the 7.62mm L7A2.

A few changes have been made in its design, particularly in the barrel. In addition, a tripod has been developed to permit the weapon to be used in the
sustained fire role. Although almost identical to the MAG in its significant
characteristics, minor changes have been made to accommodate British
manufacturing methods and material specifications. The L7A2 has an attachment for a 50-round belt box on the left side of the receiver, double pawls and
a double bent sear with the slide machined to match.

The weapon was developed using the best points of weapons that had
already proved themselves. Both the piston and the bolt are derived from the
Browning automatic rifle. Its feed mechanism is nearly one-for-one with that

Above: Guardsmen with an L7A2 LMG version of FN's MAG.

of the German MG42 of World War II, an earlier counterpart of the MAG in the sense that both guns were widely adaptable.

The L7A2 is used in both light and medium machine-gun roles. In the LMG role it is fired from the shoulder using the bipod mount. In the MMG sustained-fire role it is mounted on the L4A1 tripod and the stock is replaced by a recoil buffer. In this configuration the L7A2 can be used either for direct fire or indirect, using the same dial sight as the 81mm mortar.

It is a popular weapon, and, while production is now complete, has been purchased in its various forms by some 20 countries, remaining in service with the British, Belgian, Dutch and some Commonwealth forces.

Below: Left-hand firing of the L7A2 GPMG.

7.62mm PK general-purpose machine gun

Origin: Soviet Union. **Type:** General-purpose machine gun. **Dimensions:** (overall) 45.7in (1,160mm), (barrel) 25.9in (658mm). **Weight:** (PK) 19.8lb (9kg), (PKM) 18.5lb (8.93kg); (tripod) 16.5lb (7.5kg); (100-round belt) 5.4lb (2.44kg). **Cartridge:** 7.62mm x 54R Soviet. **Feed:** 100-, 200-, or 250-round belts. **Muzzle velocity:** 2,706f/s (825m/s). **Effective range:** 1,094yd (1,000m). **Rate of fire:** (cyclic) 690-720rpm.

The *Pulemyot Kalashnikova* (PK) family is an excellent series of weapons first seen in 1964, which are effectively the first Soviet GPMGs. Unlike almost all other Soviet rifle-caliber weapons, except the Dragunov 7.62mm SVD snipers' rifle, they fire the long 7.62mm x 54 rimmed cartridge, with over twice the propellant charge of the standard nature, a feature which illustrates the surprising lack of 'standardisation' in Soviet ammunition.

The PK is a fully automatic, gas-operated weapon. It incorporates what, at first sight, appears to be a hotch-potch of design features from other weapons. The rotating bolt is a Kalashnikov design (as used in the AK-47 and RPK), the cartridge extractor and barrel-change are Goryunov (as used in the

SGM), the feed system is derived from that in the Czechoslovak Model 52 LMG, and finally the trigger is a Degtyarev design (as used in the RPD). It is, nonetheless, an excellent weapon.

There is a large variety of versions. The PK is the basic gun, weighing some 19.8lb (9kg), with a forward-mounted bipod; it is the standard squad weapon throughout the Soviet Army and Naval Infantry. On a dual-purpose, light tripod, it is designated the PKS and is used in either the sustained fire role, or, with the tripod having been opened up, as a light AA weapon. The PKT is a solenoid-operated version without sights, stock or trigger mechanism for use as a coaxially mounted weapon in armored vehicles. The PKM is the latest service version; it is lighter in weight (18.5lb (8.39kg)) with unfluted barrel and hinged butt rest; on a tripod it is designated the PKMS. A pintle-mounted version with twin spade-grips instead of the stock and the normal trigger group replaced by a butterfly trigger is designated the PKMB. This is designed for pintle mounting on armored vehicles.

Continuing the high standard of excellence to be found in the great majority of Soviet small arms, the PK series is in wide-scale use throughout the Soviet armed forces, the Warsaw Pact and Soviet client states. It is used by special forces such as the Soviet Paratroops and Naval Infantry.

Below: The 7.62mm PK series of LMGs is still in wide-scale use with Soviet forces, including paratroops and naval infantry. This is the LMG version but there are many others for use as HMGs or AAMGs.

RPG series

Origin: Soviet Union. **Type:** Anti-tank rocket launchers. **Dimensions:**
Length RPG-7V (less projectile) 38.5in (990mm); RPG-18 (folded) 27.75in
(705mm), (extended) 39.4in (1,000mm). **Weight:** RPG-7V (less projectile)
15.42lb (7kg), RPG-18 (complete) 8.8lb (4kg). **Projectile:** RPG-7V weight
4.96lb (2.25kg); diameter 3.35in (85mm); RPG-18 weight 5.5lb (2.5kg);
diameter 2.5in (64mm). **Muzzle velocity:** RPG-7V 984f/s (300m/s);
RPG-18 374f/s (114m/s). **Effective range:** RPG-7V 328yd (300m); RPG-18
219yd (200m). **Armor penetration:** RPG-7V 12in (320mm).

The Soviet Army has placed great emphasis on anti-tank defence since its
traumatic experiences at the hands of the German Panzer troops during World
War II. For many years the standard anti-armor weapon of the Soviet infantry
and marines has been the RPG-7V (RPG = *Reaktivniy Protivotankovyi
Granatomet* (rocket, anti-tank grenade launcher)). This weapon fires a projectile whose internal rocket motor ignites a short distance from the muzzle, sus-
taining flight out to about 550yd (500m).

The HEAT warhead has good anti-armor performance, being capable of
penetrating 12.6in (320mm) of conventional armor. However, the large, slow-

Above: RPG-7 (this is a Chinese version) is a small weapon which has proved very popular with terrorists around the world.

Left: Soldier inserts the grenade into the muzzle of the launcher. Grenade weighs 4.96lb (2.25kg), launcher 15.42lb (7kg).

Below: RPG-7 in firing position. The missile is reasonably accurate, but is very sensitive and erratic in cross-winds.

flying projectile is extremely susceptible to cross-winds and its accuracy depends to a very large degree upon the skill of the operator in estimating wind effects. The standard optical sight is frequently supplemented by the NSP-2 (IR) night sight. There is also a folding version, designated RPG-7D, which was originally intended for use by airborne troops.

Both RPG-7V and RPG-7D are standard issue for Soviet and Warsaw Pact forces, and are also widely used by Third World forces and a number of terrorist organisations. Even in the hands of unskilled and illiterate troops they are highly effective against bunkers and buildings, vehicles of all types, and even under certain favourable circumstances, helicopters, but within the cross-wind limitation described above.

A new weapon, designated RPG-16, has recently appeared with Soviet Paratroop units, which appears to be a product-improved RPG-7V. This weapon has a permanently fitted bipod, and the rocket is not carried on the weapon, as is the case with RPG-7V. It has been suggested that the RPG-16 projectile may work on the double-warhead principle: the first shaped-charge makes the initial penetration of the target's armor, following which the second charge is fired through to exploit the damage caused by the first.

The RPG-18 is a disposable light anti-armor weapon (LAW), which has just entered service. The launcher is a telescopic, extruded-alloy tube, which is 27.75in (705mm) long in the carrying mode. The launcher is pulled out to its full length of 39.4in (1,000mm) before firing. The launch tube has a series of simple drawings, giving the operating instructions, an idea apparently derived from the US M72 LAW.

Above: Afghan mujahideen with an RPG-16, a product-improved RPG-7, captured from occupying Soviet forces.

Below: Vietnamese soldier with an RPG-2, the earlier version of the RPG-7. Thousands of the RPG-2/7 family are in use.

LAW80 Light anti-tank weapon

Origin: United Kingdom. **Type:** Portable anti-tank weapon. **Dimensions:** Length 3.3ft (1m) folded; 4.95ft (1.5m) extended; caliber 3.7in (94mm). **Weights:** Carry 21.1lb (9.6kg); shoulder 19.3lb (8.8kg). **Penetration:** Greater than 2.4in (600mm) of armor. **Range:** 22-500yd (20-500m).

The LAW80 is a one-shot, low cost, disposable, short-range anti-tank weapon system. It is designed to permit the operator to engage main battle tanks over short ranges with the high probability of a hit.

It is stored and transported holding 24 launchers and issued directly to the user; it is fully man-portable with personal weapons and pack with carrying handle and shoulder sling.

A spotting rifle is used with the system, which contains five rounds — which can be fired without revealing position. The 9mm ammunition, which is matched ballistically to the main projectile, is marked by a tracer and by a flash head to record a hit on a hard target. The operator can select and fire the main projectile at any time.

The LAW80 sight has its own sliding protective cover. End caps provide sealing for the tubes against immersion, despite the fact that the projectile itself is sealed. After removal of the end caps, the HEAT projectile is extended rearwards from the outer tube. The launch tube is automatically locked into position and the sight erected.

The gunner then only has to select "arm" on a lever to use the trigger to fire either the spotting rifle or the projectile. A non-electric system made up of a percussion cap in the launcher connected by a flash tube to the rocket igniter fires the projectile.

Below: The LAW80, a lightweight, man-portable, short-range anti-tank weapon, also has a role in special forces operations.

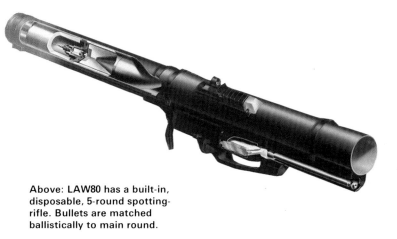

Above: LAW80 has a built-in, disposable, 5-round spotting-rifle. Bullets are matched ballistically to main round.

A HEAT warhead and its flying unit make up the forward part of the projec-tile, and there is a double-ogive nose-switch, which also provides the op-timum standoff distance from the target. At the rear of the projectile the com-posite aluminium and filament-wound motor-case has an extruded vane pro-pellant. Four fins are mounted on the rear of the motor.

In the British armed forces the weapon is used by infantry, supporting arms, Royal Marines, and the RAF Regiment. Some special operations personnel claim the LAW80 is used as anything but an anti-tank weapon; they describe it as a "super bullet", and as a device that comes under the heading of an "attention-getter" for tanks.

Below: British Marines storm ashore from a landing-craft. One carries LAW80 with ease showing its excellent man-portability.

Stinger, FIM-92A

Origin: United States. **Type:** Man-portable air defence missile.
Dimensions: Missile length 60in (1,524mm); body diameter 2.75in
(69.8mm). **Weights:** Launch 24lb (10.9kg); package 35lb (15.8kg).
Propulsion: Atlantic Research. **Guidance:** Optical aiming, IR homing.
Range: In excess of 3.1 miles (5km). **Flight speed:** About Mach 2.
Warhead: High explosive.

This successor to the first-generation Redeye missile went to the field in
Europe in 1982. Stinger has a much improved infra-red guidance system over
the Redeye that permits effective attack from all angles, whereas Redeye was
limited to a stern chase. Stinger also has greater resistance to countermeasures and incorporates an IFF system for positive identification of hostile
aircraft, a capability considered essential by friendly aircrew who are increasingly apprehensive of the sophisticated air defence weapons issued to their
own troops. The IFF device, about the size of the average canteen, is attached
to the firer's belt. The missile is issued as a certified round of ammunition in a
disposable sealed launching tube, which is attached to the gripstock tracking
unit containing the missile's controls and pre-launch electronics.

   To improve its effectiveness and cope with ECM of the future, an advanced
seeker called Stinger POST (for Passive Optical Seeker Technique) has been
developed. It was introduced on the production line with the Fiscal 1983 buy.
This version operates in both the ultraviolet and the infra-red spectra. The improved missile reached the field in Fiscal 1987.

   Stingers are being used by the anti-Soviet forces in Afghanistan with, by all
accounts, deadly effect. The Soviets are now fighting that war at greater and
safer distances . . . fearing this weapon in the hands of the mujahideen.

**Right: The US Stinger man-portable, air defense missile has proved
effective in the Falklands and in Afghanistan.**

**Below: In conventional war the radioman is needed to prevent own
aircraft being hit, but would not be required in SF operations.**

Blowpipe/Javelin

Origin: United Kingdom. **Type:** Surface-to-air missile (SAM). **Canister:** Length 54.7in (1.390m); weight: 48.3lb (21.9kg). **Missile:** Length 54.7in (1,390mm); diameter: 3in (76mm). **Rocket motor:** Two-stage, solid-fuel. **Effective range:** 3 to 3.7 miles (5 to 6km). **Flight speed:** Supersonic.

Blowpipe is a lightweight, supersonic, self-contained SAM system, currently used by 14 armed forces in 10 countries. The system worked well in the 1982 South Atlantic war (it was deployed by both sides) and a number of successes were recorded. It has also found its way to Afghanistan, being reported in use by the mujahideen from 1983 onwards.

The basic Blowpipe system comprises two units. The first is a sealed launch canister containing the missile, which is treated in the supply system simply as a round of ammunition. Second is the aiming unit, a self-contained pack. To prepare for action the aiming unit is clipped to the launch canister, and the complete system is then put on the operator's shoulder. When the operator has acquired the target and confirmed it as hostile he pulls the trigger, generating electrical impulses which energise the thermal battery, powering up the aiming unit and one second later firing the missile motor. The missile is ejected from the tube by the first-stage motor and, when well clear of the operator, the second-stage ignites. The operator then 'gathers' the missile and guides it to the target using a thumb-stick, which transmits signals by a radio link to the missile.

The latest service version is the Javelin, which uses the Blowpipe missile, but with a more powerful motor which significantly reduces the time of flight. The aiming unit is externally similar to that for Blowpipe, but houses a new control system, using semi-automatic command line-of-sight (SACLOS) guidance in which all the operator needs to do is keep the cross-wires in his sight on the target. The TV camera in the aiming unit tracks the flare in the missile tail and compares this with the signals from the sight; any mismatch is converted into an error correction signal which is transmitted to the missile.

Javelin is man-portable but installations are under development for both soft-skinned and armored vehicles.

Above: The Blowpipe air defense missile has been sold to many overseas customers, including special forces.

Left: Successor to Blowpipe, Javelin is much faster, with SACLOS guidance system, greatly reducing the load on the operator.

SA-7 Grail

Origin: Soviet Union. **Type:** Surface-to-air missile (SAM). **Launcher:**
Length 53.25in (1.35m); weight: 23.4lb (10.6kg). **Missile:** Length 48.8in
(1,240mm); diameter 2.75in (70mm); weight 20.3lb (9.2kg). **Rocket
motor:** Three-stage, solid-fuel. **Effective height:** SA-7A maximum 9,843ft
(3,000m); minimum 164ft (50m). SA-7B maximum 16,000ft (5km);
minimum 164ft (50m). **Maximum speed:** SA-7A 994mph (1,600km/h).
SA-7B 1,242mph (2,000km/h).

Originally called *Strela* (Arrow) in the West, this widely used SAM is now
designated the SA-7, and has the NATO reporting name of 'Grail'. It is a simple infantry weapon and originally had great similarity with the US Redeye,
sharing many of the latter's notorious shortcomings. Most important of these
was the inability of the uncooled PbS infra-red seeker to lock onto any heat
source on a fixed-wing target, other than the tailpipe. This limited
engagements to 'tail chases', which was obviously tactically unacceptable.
They could, however, hit helicopters from almost any angle.

**Right: Soviet air defense missileman launches an SA-7 from the rear
hatch of a BMP APC during a training exercise.**

**Below: SA-7 is used by Warsaw Pact military forces, Soviet client
states and numerous terrorist organizations.**

The SA-7 missile is essentially a tube with a dual-thrust solid-fuel motor, steered by canard fins. The operator merely aims the launcher at the target using the open sight and takes the first pressure on the trigger, which switches on the thermal battery. He then waits for an audible warning and the red light to turn green, which indicate that the seeker has locked-on; he then applies the full trigger pressure. The boost charge fires and burns out before the tail of the missile has cleared the tube. At a safe distance the sustainer motor ignites, accelerating the missile to about Mach 1.5.

The 5.5lb (2.5kg) warhead has a smooth fragmentation casing, and is fitted with both impact and grazing fuzes. The original warhead was lethal only against small aircraft and in the Yom Kippur war almost half the Israeli A-4s hit by SA-7s returned to base.

An improved missile (SA-7B) has been in production since 1972 with augmented propulsion giving a higher speed and better maximum operating height. It also has an infra-red filter to screen out decoys and the prominent nose ring on the front-end of the launcher is believed to house a much better guidance system.

There are probably 50,000 missiles and almost as many launchers in service, large numbers of them in use by terrorists.

THE MOST fundamental questions concerning special forces are why are they needed, who are they, and what do they do? They are, after all, expensive to select, train and equip, and their very élitism and aura of secrecy tend to induce envy in other sections of their armies and fear in governments. Nevertheless, many countries now see little alternative but to have such groups.

There have long been special units in many forces, which have set particular conditions for entry. These have varied from simple matters such as height for 'guards' units, to a very high degree of physical fitness for parachute and marine units. Starting in the late 1950s, however, the needs of counter-revolutionary warfare (CRW) gave rise to a requirement for units with a high degree of skill and specialisation in dealing with specific threats. This expanded slowly in the 1960s until the spread of international terrorism and the prevalence of hijacking, kidnapping, random bombings and murders forced a marked upsurge in the numbers and size of special forces.

Special forces tend to operate in the area that lies between the police and the 'heavy' infantry. Some countries have tried to fill this gap by developing special sections of the police. In West Germany, for example, the special force GSG-9 (GSG = Grenszschutzgruppe = Border Defence Group) is part of the State Border Police, directed by the Federal Ministry of the Interior. In the United Kingdom the equivalent is the Special Air Service (SAS) Regiment, which is a unit of the British Army, although various police forces have started to create their own armed squads, albeit dealing with lower level situations than would be dealt with by the SAS.

These forces operate in situations where police cannot, either

Left: Federal German Police lined up for anti-riot duties with helmets, shields and body armor, invaluable for today's police.

Above: Black-clad special forces soldier abseiling with MP5. He must be at instant readiness for long periods for operations anywhere in the world.

for legal or training reasons. They are always at a high degree of readiness and are trained and equipped to deal with a wide range of contingencies. These can be conveniently divided into three levels. At the first, or lowest, level is the operation against a small number of terrorists in a fairly confined target such as an aircraft, ship or single building, and located either in the home country or in a friendly territory with full cooperation from the authorities. Examples of such operations are the British SAS rescue of the hostages in the Iranian Embassy siege (1980) and the West German rescue of the hostages in the hijacking at Mogadishu (1977). The second level of special force operations are those involving an attack against larger targets at long distances and in which the enemy are either terrorists supported by regular troops or regular troops themselves. Examples of this type are the Israeli rescue of the hijacked hostages at Entebbe (1976) and the US Operation Eagle Claw in which the Delta Force attempted to rescue the US hostages in Teheran (1980). Finally, there are the third level operations in a proper war setting where special forces act as a specialist part of the regular military forces. Examples of this are the US raid to release the prisoners of war held at Son Tay in 1970 and the British SAS and SBS (Special Boat Squadron, an élite element of the Royal Marines) operations in the South Atlantic war of 1982.

General tactics

Perhaps the highest profile activity of special forces is hostage rescue. For some years after aircraft hijacking was invented it appeared to be an insuperable tactic, and the balance of advantage seemed to lie irretrievably with the terrorist. At first confined to aircraft, hijacking has since taken place on trains, buses and even ships. However, the authorities in most countries have managed to develop suitable responses, which have led to a marked decrease, although the complexity of modern transportation systems, coupled with the difficulty of maintaining the necessary high level of vigilance, means that such crimes remain a constant possibility.

Below: Hostage takers increasingly hide in buildings in urban areas, giving rescuers considerable problems in achieving rapid and effective entry.

In all counter-terrorist operations the first essential is intelligence; indeed, good intelligence should enable incidents to be prevented altogether. Long-term, in-depth intelligence is necessary and it would appear that a great number of military and police authorities now exchange intelligence on an international scale, which has proved to be a major deterrent to many would-be terrorists. Once an incident has started, however, there are two requirements: first, to gather all possible intelligence on the group involved, their personalities, motives, tactics, doctrines and determination, leading to an analysis of their strengths and weaknesses. Second, to establish everything possible about the actual incident itself: how many are involved, what arms they have, what their contacts are, how many hostages there are and so on. From all this contingency plans can be

prepared to cover various possible situations and then it is a matter of waiting.

When the actual operation takes place the essentials are surprise, determination and rapid, coordinated action. Overwhelming force is seldom necessary; indeed, in many situations (eg, an attack on an aircraft) it may not be physically possible to get too many men into the target area. Two good examples of the tactics involved are the Israeli rescue mission to Entebbe and the British breaking of the Iranian Embassy siege in London.

Entebbe Operation

The Israeli rescue operation at Entebbe was a classic of its kind, showing the ability of special forces to react quickly to unexpected crises, to make rapid but flexible plans and to operate at considerable distance from their home base. The crisis began at 1210 hours on 27 June 1976, when an Air France Airbus (Flight AF 139) was hijacked en route from Athens to Paris. The flight had started in Tel Aviv and there were many Jews among

Above: SAS 'enemy' (left) is captured in a recent desert exercise. The SAS were formed during World War II in the North African desert campaign.

the 254 passengers. The pilot pressed the 'hijack alert' button as he turned for Benghazi under orders from the leader of the combined Baader-Meinhof/Palestinian group, led by a German, Wilfried Boese. The aircraft refuelled at Benghazi and then flew to its destination Entebbe, Uganda, which was at that time under the erratic rule of 'Field Marshal' Idi Amin.

Israeli planners had many problems, including shortage of time, paucity of information, and distance. There was also the problem of the non-Jewish hostages. Some of these problems solved themselves. The hijackers released the non-Jewish hostages (although the Air France crew insisted that they stay with the remaining Jewish hostages), intelligence on Entebbe and the situation there began to trickle in, and Kenya agreed to the use of Nairobi airport.

The rescue plan was approved by the Israeli Prime Minister early on 3 July and a dress-rehearsal was carried out later that morning, taking just 55 minutes from aircraft touch-down to take-off with simulated rescued hostages. At 1600 hours that afternoon four C-130 aircraft took off for the flight to Entebbe; they were followed some two hours later by two Boeing 707 aircraft one of which was a flying command post, the other a mobile hospital. The hospital aircraft flew to Nairobi airport but,

Below: A very cheerful C-130 pilot is thanked by hostages who had lived through days of terror in Entebbe, held by a PLO group supported by Idi Amin.

in the event, its facilities were not in fact required.

The four C-130s landed at Entebbe at 0001 hours, the first going straight to the control tower, which was captured before the airfield landing lights could be switched off. Another party blew up a number of Ugandan Air Force MiG fighters in a noisy diversion (which also ensured that the fighters could not follow the Israelis after they took off for home). Another group set up ambushes on the approach road to the airport to ensure that no Ugandan rescue forces could interrupt the operation.

The preliminaries successfully completed, the signal was given to assault the terminal building where the hostages were held.

The terrorist leader behaved somewhat indecisively and was killed as he returned into the building, his German female accomplice being shot outside the building. Inside the terminal the assaulting troops yelled at the hostages to keep down but three hostages were shot by stray bullets as the last of the terrorists were being killed. The terrorists disposed of, the released hostages were rapidly shepherded out to the waiting C-130s, and at this point the assault force commander, Lieutenant-Colonel 'Yoni' Netanyahu, was shot and killed by a single shot from a Ugandan soldier in a nearby building.

The first C-130 took off at 0045 hours and the fourth at 0054 hours. The cost of the whole operation was one member of the rescue force killed and three wounded; three hostages were killed during the assault and one, Mrs Dora Bloch, who had earlier been taken to a Ugandan hospital, was murdered by Ugandans in revenge for the humiliating débâcle. All the terrorists were killed, together with 20 Ugandans.

The operation was a brilliant success, confirming the Israeli reputation for rapid and determined action.

Below: 4 July 1976 and an Israeli Air Force C-130 Hercules lands at Lod Airport, carrying the hostages who had been freed in the spectacular raid on Entebbe.

Iranian Embassy Siege

A second example of a classic special force operation was the 1980 rescue of the hostages in the Iranian Embassy in London. Its impact lay in the fact that it took place in full view of the media and was the first public display of the long-suspected prowess of the British Special Air Service (SAS).

The Embassy was taken over at 1130 hours on 30 April 1980 by six terrorists armed with three 9mm automatic pistols, one 0.38in revolver and some hand grenades. The six men were seeking independence for Arabistan, an area of southern Iran, which has a long record of

Below: London Iranian Embassy siege; a hostage flees across the balconies. The speed and efficiency of the 11 minute rescue operation stunned watchers.

resistance to northern domination. This was an internal Iranian dispute, in which the British had no involvement whatsoever. There were 29 people in the Embassy at the time of the takeover (4 British and 22 Iranian, 3 of the latter escaping in the first few minutes). Having stated their demands and set a deadline (1200 hours, 1 May) the terrorists found themselves involved in continuous contact with the police, discussing the release of sick hostages, postponement of deadlines and passing messages to and from third parties. This was all part of a recognised police gambit to establish and maintain contact, to set up relationships between police officers and individual terrorists, and to begin the long process of wearing the terrorists down. Meanwhile every element of the exterior of the building was being

investigated in minute detail to establish possible entry routes.

By the third day there had been numerous contacts and the terrorists agreed to release two hostages in return for a radio broadcast giving a statement of their aims. Both were achieved and the police sent in a meal. The siege continued through Days 4 and 5, but on Day 6 the terrorists

Above: London firemen ready to extinguish fires started accidentally during the rescue. The position of the Iranians in Embassy Row is clearly shown.

were noticeably more edgy and at 1330 hours the leader shot and killed one of the Embassy staff, the body being pushed out onto the pavement at 1900 hours.

Above: After its success in World War II the SAS was disbanded, only to be reformed in the 1950s to fight terrorists in Malaya. They proved as successful in jungle as they had been in the African desert.

The SAS assault took place just 26 minutes later, using 12 men, in the usual SAS four-man teams. Everything that could be done to heighten the impact was done: the soldiers were dressed from head to foot in black, even including anti-gas respirators,

and looked extremely menacing. They were armed with a variety of weapons, including Heckler & Koch MP5 carbines and Browning 9mm pistols. Tear gas was used together with 'stun' grenades, while the explosion of the shaped charges added to the noise and confusion. The SAS men had, naturally, pored over the plans of the 50-room building in minute detail and had spent many hours studying the photographs of the hostages. Just before the assault started the police spoke to the terrorists

on the telephone to distract their attention at the critical moment.

One element of the assault was made from the roof, the men abseiling down ropes at the front and rear of the building, the second from the balcony of the adjacent building. At the rear the third soldier became entangled in the rope and had to be cut down, falling onto a balcony. At the front the men climbed onto a balcony of the Iranian Embassy, placed a shaped charge and entered. Inside there was chaos, with noise of firearms, flashes, bangs, shouts and yells. The terrorists managed to wound a few of the hostages before they were all killed by the SAS, except for one who managed to hide among the rescued hostages for a few minutes before being detected and arrested.

The entire operation took 11 minutes and established the SAS's reputation globally. It also delivered an inescapable message to other terrorists: that any future adventure in the UK would be dealt with in a similar manner.

COMBAT ammunition can be divided into three separate categories — military, police and special forces — each meeting a distinctly different set of parameters. The Geneva and Hague conventions specify the type of ammunition allowed in a conflict between nations, the reason being a humane desire to inflict as little injury as possible. In fact, cynics point out that a man killed on the battlefield can be ignored by his companions, but a wounded man needs at least two other active participants to evacuate him, plus an estimated seven rear-echelon people needed to transport and hospitalise him afterwards.

The standard military criterion is *reliability* in all climatic conditions. In guns which are often badly maintained and which are (in the case of NATO or other multi-nation armed forces) weapons other than that for which the round was specifically made, the only suitable round to fulfil this criterion is ball. This is a fully jacketed, round-nosed or spire-pointed bullet with sufficient power and weight to operate in a variety of weapons.

The second category of combat round is designed for the police, to meet very different rules. While not intended for international usage, the advice of official British experts is taken seriously the world over, not least that of the Working Party of the British Home Office on firearms who have specified the ideal police round. The Home Office criteria are as follows:
1. Maximum speed of incapacitation.
2. Minimum penetration.
3. Minimum richochet.
4. Minimum lead pollution.
5. Non-expansion in the human body.

Numbers 1 to 3 are good tactical considerations in urban conflict, with the possibility of an innocent passerby being endangered. Point 4 is simply a training consideration, but point 5 is where the problems start. Simply stated, maximum speed of incapacitation and non-expansion in the human body are exact opposites. To achieve one you must lose the other, except in absolutely ideal laboratory conditions.

Most European nations have similar restraints, in fact one northern European police force has a directive specifically stating that "A felon should be incapacitated with firearms by shooting him in the legs".

Special forces ammunition has the least political and moral restrictions of all ammunition

Below: Some current shotgun cartridges. Of the rifled slugs in the bottom row, numbers 1, 3 and 5 are tungsten penetrators.

Above: More shotgun cartridges. SPAS round (right) is a discarding sabot tungsten carbide slug which can penetrate the side of an APC!

types, the paramount consideration being stopping power. The operation which special forces personnel are normally involved in is close-range reactive combat where the immediate neutralisation of the enemy is paramount and it is likely that further hostages or innocent bystanders could be killed if the enemy is not stopped immediately.

Special forces tend to go in cold, often outnumbered by their targets, and without 'softening up' (other than psychologically) beforehand. In these circumstances special forces need state-of-the-art training and equipment, which includes the most effective ammunition possible.

Unfortunately almost all modern high-tech weapons suitable for close quarter battle (CQB) operations are 9mm, which seems acceptable, as statistically more people are killed by 9mm than by any other caliber in modern warfare. The problem is, however, that although 9mm kills it does not stop, one example being a police incident in the USA where two officers engaged a felon with Smith and Wesson M59 9mm pistols and after shooting him 33 times he stopped!

New 9mm 'stopping' rounds

As a result, major ammunition manufacturing nations have all produced ammunition designed to give the 9mm a stopping capability. The first attempt was to produce a higher velocity, thin-jacketed, hollow-point bullet, one of the first being the American Super Vel. This round had some successes but was very high pressure and tended to misfeed in standard weapons.

There are basic ballistic problems inherent in 9mm which the ammunition manufacturers were trying to overcome. The 9mm round was designed to operate in a reciprocating machine, which required a smooth, tapered round with no sharp angles or other blemishes and small enough to fit into the butt of a pistol, but powerful enough to operate a sub-machine gun. The 9mm Parabellum was all of these things, but, because of the necessary bullet configuration in shape, weight and velocity, it tends to pass straight through the intended target!

Stopping power can be enhanced by five methods. First by enlarging the projectile. Obviously, the larger the diameter of the bullet the more damage it will do. This option is not possible, as 9mm is the caliber and any increase requires either a retrograde step to .45 ACP (ie, a Thompson or Ingram), or it would mean having to build a gun around the mythical 'perfect caliber'. Both these solutions would entail serious resupply problems in the field.

The second possible answer is to use a bullet with good wound channel capabilities. Former American small arms ammunition developer Elmer Kieth developed the semi-wad cutter bullet for precisely this reason. Instead of the wound channel simply closing behind the bullet, a core is cut out which causes the subject to lose blood much more quickly, and the damage to major organs is usually more severe. The major problem with this approach is an unacceptably high percentage of failures to feed.

Third, hollow- or soft-point bullets which are designed to expand on impact, thus increasing the diameter of the projectile sufficiently to cause it to stop in the body. Or, if it does pass through, the increased size will ensure that most of the energy is transferred, causing a corresponding increase in damage to body issue. This system is used in almost all rifle rounds used for hunting purposes and is totally effective. The problem with pistol caliber is that the velocity is too low to guarantee bullet deformation. Lightweight, high-velocity hollow points have been tried but their main problem is that if the jacket is weak enough to rupture effectively on soft targets, a wallet or any item of military kit could break up the bullet before it can do any damage.

Fourth, frangibility (bullet break-up), but unfortunately this effect depends on which area of the body the projectile hits. Even under the best conditions the energy can be dissipated on cover rather than the target and the .223 rifle round, which has a relatively thin jacket, has been known to break up on small twigs and long grass!

Finally, there is the 'Plus P', in which velocity is increased and weight decreased to achieve higher kinetic energy. This is the most effective of the original methods used to increase stopping power, since the lighter bullet tended to slow down quicker, which often caused it to stop in the body, transferring all its energy. The successes gained by the application of kinetic energy rather than momentum caused the ballistic experts to attempt to define the perfect stopping round. The parameters were:

1. Totally reliable.
2. High energy dump.
3. No shoot-through.
4. Ability to defeat basic body armor.
5. Low recoil.
6. No richochet.

At first glance these requirements seem almost unobtainable, and they certainly are if standard bullet design is used, but there are now many types of what are called 'fourth generation rounds'. These rounds can be divided into two main categories: the first is frangibility; the second is AET (accelerated energy transfer) profile.

There are three contenders in the first category. The Glaser Safety Slug is well established and has excellent stopping power. As said earlier, 87 per cent of people shot with small arms survive, yet to date over 90 per cent of the people shot with Glaser have died. This phenomenal increase in stopping power is achieved by using the

Below: Pistol rounds varying from .22 (bottom right) to .44 caliber (second from right, bottom), and from roundnose (third from left, bottom) to Splat polymer/metal mix (top, fifth from left, upper).

bullet's energy in the most efficient way possible.

The construction of the bullet is the secret: it is similar to a shotgun charge encapsulated in a thin cupronickel jacket with a plastic cap at the front to seal the shot in, and is fired at about 1,800f/s. When it hits an uneven surface or a semi-liquid medium, the cap ruptures, spilling the No 12 shot out of the bullet. As a sphere has the largest surface area of any object of a given size, the shot gives up its energy into the target eight times faster than if the bullet had stayed intact. This speed of energy transfer causes massive systemic shock and stops the subject almost instantly.

Glaser has three problem areas, however. The first is its cost: between $3 and $4.5 (£2 and £3) per round. Secondly, if a hostage or non-combatant is hit, they are dead. More important is that, if the hostile is hiding behind a hostage, there is no ability to shoot through the hostage to engage the enemy. Finally, and most important, the round is totally defeated by any form of angled cover; even an internal softwood door causes the bullet to break up if hit at under 80 per cent from true.

There is, however, a special round which is black-tipped, as against the blue for the standard round. This is designed for police and military use, and has some body armor and angle penetration capabilities.

The second round in this category is 'Spartan', which is made in Britain as a training round. It is designed to break up on impact with a steel back stop, and not to over-penetrate or travel too far. These characteristics are achieved by producing a bullet made from a lead dust and polymer mix, pressure-moulded into the required shape. This idea was first started with the .22 short Gallery ammunition which is still used in funfairs.

Some of this 'training' am-

Above: Used by many special forces Glaser rounds (l to r — 7.62mm, .44 Magnum, .38, 9mm) are designed for stopping power. Ninety percent of those shot by such rounds die.

munition was sent to one of the UK's special forces units and they immediately realised its potential. Basically, the human body is made of two very hard substances, bone and tissue with a high water content. Bone is obviously hard but flesh is soft. Consider the properties of water: it is incompressible, which is why it is used in hydraulics. If a high-velocity round hits water (ie, a person) the water cannot move out of the way quickly enough for the bullet, and it cannot be compressed. Something has to give, and the bullet which is designed to break up does exactly that!

This round is still in its development stage, but it looks promising. The only problem inherent to its design concept is that it will never fulfil all the 'fourth generation' criteria as the velocity cannot be pushed up high enough due to its lead content making the weight too high.

The final round which fits into this category is a direct development of the 'Spartan' round, called 'Splat'. As with 'Spartan', it is a metal and polymer mix, but it has two important differences. First, the metal content, both in volume and in weight, is designed to produce in excess of 1,800f/s and certain break-up in the human body. Second, the profile of this bullet is desig͟ to allow it to penetrate medium cover *without* breaking up until it exits the far side. This is an enormous advance over both 'Glaser' and the 'Spartan' rounds.

It has two other distinct advantages. It retails at approximately the same low price as standard ball, and it is non-lead. This is important for training in non-range areas, since lead pollution is a serious hazard for both the military and police who shoot regularly.

The AET profile round is the second category of 'fourth generation' round. The first effective round of this type was developed for .38 revolvers, and is basically a hollow base wad cutter loaded into the case upside down! The expansion properties of such a bullet were high, to say the least.

In an attempt to improve the penetration by controlling the rate of expansion and enhancing the strength of the projectile, a steel pin was swaged into the center of the hollow. This tended to have the interesting effect of producing two projectiles — one lead, which expanded and stopped quickly, and the other steel, which punched through the target. This had an extra advantage in that the steel pin tended to defeat some body armor.

In recent years the round has been produced in many other calibers, both for revolvers and automatics, including the 9mm. The only known problem is reliability. The weapon has to receive specialist gunsmithing (barrel porting) to accept this round for total reliability, which is an unacceptable condition for military use.

It took 10 years or more to produce the next AET round, of which numerous versions are available, including Geco action, CBX, Equalloy, KTW and THV. The first type, which is made ⸱⸱rmany, is 'Geco action' ⸱⸱T' in the USA), which ⸱⸱w bullet with a ⸱⸱e round is

fired the core is displaced, falling away from the bullet within a short distance from the barrel. When the bullet hits the target, its construction makes it tumble, causing high tissue damage, and the bullet is retained within the body, ensuring a high-energy transfer. The only problem noted to date is a failure to penetrate angled cover.

The second type of AET round, 'Equalloy', is made in England. At the moment it is designed only for revolvers but it has an application in the anti-hijack role on aircraft. The bullet, made from an aluminium alloy, is extremely lightweight and to enable it to attain sufficient velocity in the weapon, the bearing surface of the bullet is almost twice as long as a standard round. A nylon coating is used to ensure a good seal and to stop the aluminium from depositing in the barrel. On test 2,050f/s was recorded, but it was still possible to get the bullet to stop in 3.5in of Swedish soap (human tissue substitute)!

The third type of AET profile round is 'THV', a totally new concept, considered to be as close to the 'perfect round' as possible. The ballistic phenomenon used is a 'reverse ogive', where the forward sec-

Below: Fourth generation Accelerated Energy Transfer rounds with reverse ogive. Their concave cutting edges increase effects on the human target.

tion of the bullet protrudes beyond the case. This profile causes the cutting area hitting the target to be concave rather than convex, which has an effect on the body similar to that of a 'belly-flop' to a diver. As discussed earlier, hydraulic effect can be used to transfer energy in the target, as long as the velocity is high enough. With this projectile, not only is the velocity high enough at 2,500f/s, but it also has the effect of transferring energy over a 90 degree angle throughout the bullet's path. Add to this that the construction allows good armor piercing, relatively low richochet (by comparison with standard ammunition), low recoil, good stopping power and to date no problems on functioning, and you have a near-perfect special forces round.

A number of special forces units use shotguns, normally for house clearing and similar close-range operations. There are two main reasons why the manually operated, small magazine capacity, bulky shotgun is often used rather than a compact SMG or pistol. First, stopping power. SG or 0.0. buck has 9.33 caliber soft lead balls in each cartridge, each travelling at approximately 1,300f/s (395m/s), which can be likened to a nine-round burst from a sub-machine gun being delivered at the same instant!

The second and overpowering reason is variety: a standard 12 bore/gauge shotgun can shoot a vast number of different cartridges, ranging from birdshot to grenades.

Lethal cartridges
Birdshot — close range, will not penetrate internal walls.
Small buckshot — close to medium range, 16-50ft (5-15m); will not kill non-combatants outside operational area.
Large buckshot — medium to long range, 50-130ft (15-40m); some penetration of hard cover, excellent stopping power out to

100ft (30m); gives a spread of approximately 1in per yard (25mm per metre) of range.
Rifled slug — medium to long range, 50-165ft (15-50m), very high penetration of hard cover, excellent stopping power; must be point aimed.
TC armor-piercing slug — all the characteristics of rifled slug, plus ability to penetrate *all* soft body armor and most light armored vehicles.
BRI slug — gives rifle-like accuracy to extend the combat range to 655ft (200m) plus.
HE slug (high explosive) — gives the ability to neutralise a room or car at 330ft (100m) plus.

Non-lethal tactical cartridges
Hatton round — specially developed to blow hinges off doors without injuring the occupants of the room.
CS Ferret — used to fill a room or car with CS gas.
Flares — signalling purposes.
Incendiary — diversionary fires, destroying vehicles, etc.
Rubber ball — riot control, long range.
Rubber SC — riot control, medium range.
Plastic birdshot — riot control, close range.

With this amount of choice, the operative can arm himself to suit the scenario, taking into account all the tactical requirements for the specific set of circumstances he has to deal with.

The major problem with the shotgun is the bulk and shape of the ammunition. The area taken by 50 rounds of 12 bore is approximately the same as 600 rounds of 9mm. Secondly, special forces can only use a manually operated shotgun, rather than a semi or fully automatic version. This is due to the shape of the cartridges, and the relatively low pressure produced, being insufficient to cause a gas blow-back system to operate reliably each time.

ALTHOUGH usually more associated with terrorists, like other esoteric devices, silenced weapons can have a place in special forces' armories. The noises generated by a firearm are composed of three elements. First and most significant is muzzle blast; second is the sound generated by the bullet's passage through the air; and third is the noise generated by the movement of the mechanical parts in automatic and semi-automatic firearms.

Muzzle blast is the result of the expansion of the hot, high pressure gases used to propel the bullet as they escape from the end of the barrel. The function of a silencer is to reduce this sound, although it should be noted that no such device ever reduces the sound to true silence and a more accurate name would be a 'sound suppressor'. How-

ever, in most modern urban environments the ambient noise level from cars, buses, trains, aircraft and radios is such that a silencer will reduce the sound of firing to a point where it is extremely difficult to detect where a bullet has come from.

These devices work on the principle of diverting the gases travelling up the barrel into a series of chambers, thus reducing the pressure at the end of the

barrel and reducing the noise. Obviously, the reduction in gas pressure at the muzzle reduces the velocity of the bullet. However, this is frequently desirable in view of the second noise source. All bullets which travel faster than the speed of sound (approximately 745mph = 1,092f/s = 333m/s) emit a sonic boom of exactly the same nature as aircraft, although in this case it is more of a 'crack' than a 'boom'. Not all bullets are supersonic in the first place, particularly those designed for pistols. The 7.65mm Browning (0.32in) round, for example, has a muzzle velocity (MV) of 984f/s (300m/s), while the British 0.38in round has an MV as low as 590f/s (180m/s).

Normal rifle bullets have very high velocities. Special ammunition is available in some calibers with a reduced charge, which brings the MV down to subsonic level, although special sights are required and effectiveness is considerably reduced. The NATO standard 7.62 round, however, has an MV of 2,750f/s (838m/s) while the new standard 5.56mm SS92 round is travelling even faster at 3,166f/s (965m/s). Some rifles can be fitted with silencers: Vaime of Finland produces one which can be fitted to almost any firearm, including rifles; it is claimed to reduce the sound of firing to that of a 0.22in rimfire weapon, whilst the silencer for 0.22in weapons is claimed to make them virtually soundless. Heckler & Koch also makes silencers for its 7.62mm G3 rifle, which screws on in place of the flash hider. It reduces the muzzle report, but as it is recom-

Left: Silenced rifles are being used increasingly by special forces. Vaime of Finland produces this sniper rifle, as well as silencer attachments for other weapons, which reduces the sound of 7.62/5.56mm weapons to that of 0.22in rimfire.

Above: An internal view of a Vaime screw-on silencer attachment. The series of baffles not only greatly reduces sound, but also eliminates muzzle-flash and reduces recoil.

Below: Heckler & Koch G3 7.62mm rifle fitted with a silencer attachment, intended mainly for use on ranges to reduce noise disturbance to local residents.

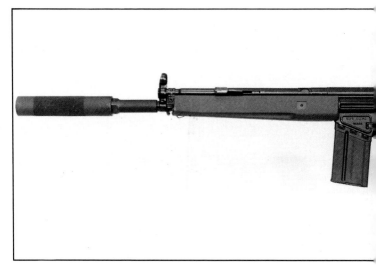

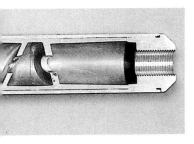

Bottom: The Chinese 7.62mm Type 64 SMG is unique in that it is designed and built as a silenced weapon; in every other case normal SMGs are fitted with silencer attachments.

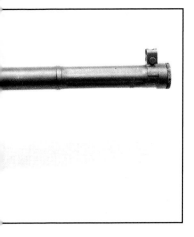

mended that subsonic ammuniton is *not* used, it is of only limited value; indeed, its stated use is for range firing to reduce the noise disturbance for nearby residents.

The 9mm Parabellum round has a normal MV of some 1,299f/s (396m/s) and thus silenced weapons using this round, particularly sub-machine guns, rely on reducing the velocity through pressure losses in the barrel.

Most silenced weapons are constructed by fitting a silencing device to an existing gun design, but the People's Republic of China has produced the 7.62mm Type 64 silenced sub-machine gun, which is unique in that it has been designed from the start as a silenced weapon. This SMG uses the 7.62mm × 25 pistol round, with a somewhat high MV of 1,683f/s (513m/s). The 7.87in (200mm) long barrel has the normal rifling grooves for the first 5in (125mm) of its length but for the next 2.4in (60mm) each groove is perforated with four rows of nine 3mm diameter holes, giving 36 holes in all, into which much of the gases escape. The outer sleeve extends a further 6.5in (165mm) beyond the end of the barrel and terminates in a muzzle cap. Between the end of the barrel and this cap is a stack of baffles, each of which is dished with a 9mm central hole; two rods pass down the baffles to keep the stacks aligned. The silencer is fairly effective and also acts as a flash suppressor. This weapon makes an interesting comparison with the British Sterling L34A1.

Mechanical noise only arises for automatic or semi-automatic weapons, self-loading weapons and, in fact, is seldom detectable more than a short distance away from the weapon. Indeed, it would be exceptional if such noise could be detected at distances greater than those from which the firer could be seen.

FOR MANY years grenades were considered to be ultra short-range weapons for the heavy infantryman, with payloads comprising either high-explosive, anti-tank or coloured smoke. The fundamental drawback was that the normal method of projection was throwing, usually by an excited, often tired and always heavily loaded infantryman. As a result they could only be used at very short ranges and were usually relatively inaccurate; not infrequently, they were as dangerous to the thrower or his comrades as to the intended target! Some armies used special devices attached to the muzzle of the standard rifle to project streamlined grenades to somewhat greater ranges, typically 110-330yd (100-300m). The other uses of the grenade were to disperse colored smoke on the battlefield or CN/CS gas in anti-riot operations. In the 1960s, however, modern technology was brought to bear on the subject, as a result of which there has been a great expansion in their use. A wide variety is available, many of them with particular applications for special forces in close-quarter combat, riot control and anti-terrorist operations.

Modern grenades are designed for one of a number of methods of projection. First (and most numerous) are grenades for throwing by hand, which are either cylindrical or egg-shaped and weigh some 9-18oz (250-500g). Their range and accuracy depend totally upon the ability of the thrower and the prevailing conditions, but a good 'shot' might be able to throw a

Below: US soldier with an M203 grenade launcher fitted to his M16A1 rifle. A single-shot device, M203 launches 40mm grenades over ranges up to 437yd (400m).

Above: Soviet AGS-17 is a purpose-built, 30mm automatic grenade launcher. Used by Soviet infantry and special forces, it is also mounted on Mi-8 HipÉ helicopters.

1lb (450g) grenade 60ft (18.3m), with an accuracy of ±3ft (1m). Some armies, particularly in the Soviet bloc, attach a small handle to the grenade to facilitate throwing.

The second means of projection is from special attachments fitted to rifles. The US M203 grenade launcher, for example, clips onto the M16 5.56mm rifle and fires 40mm grenades to an effective range against area targets of 383yd (350m) and against point targets of 164yd (150m). Such systems have the advantages of much greater range and accuracy than hand-thrown grenades, without detracting from the use and performance of the rifle. However, the grenades themselves are small and lightweight and thus have a limited payload and effect.

Specialised grenade launchers have also come into use. These vary from large caliber, single-shot pistols to automatic launchers, similar in design and size to machine guns, which can fire 40mm grenades at a rate of some

350rpm in the case of the US Mark 19 Mod 3, and 65rpm in the Soviet 30mm AGS-17. More likely to be of use to special forces are the smaller automatic grenade launchers, such as the South African 40mm Arsmcor 6-shot device, which uses the revolver principle, or the British ARWEN 37, which holds five 37mm rounds.

The grenades themselves come in a plethora of designs, the traditional model being the high-explosive, fragmentation device. Typical is the British L2A2, weighing 14oz (395g) and containing 6oz (170g) of RDX/TNT; the body is made of 0.1in (2.4m) steel wire, notched at 0.125in (3.2mm) intervals, which breaks up on explosion into several hundred pieces.

Modern technology has come to the assistance of troops and police to help in dealing with special situations such as riots, terrorist attacks and hostage-taking. For anti-riot and anti-terrorist operations one of the major weapons is the tear gas grenade, most using CS, an irritating, lachrymatory gas. As rioters now use sophisticated techniques these grenades often include devices to prevent them from simply picking the grenades up and either throwing them back or diverting them to where

their gas will have little or no effect. The Israeli Type 303 grenade deals with this problem by being made of flexible rubber; it thus bounces like a rubber ball, even when emitting gas. Other grenades burst on impact, throwing out burning CS pellets, which again cannot be thrown back.

Many special forces are used in anti-terrorist operations, especially in dealing with hijackings, where the aim is to overcome the terrorists without harming the (frequently numerous) hostages. The crucial moment is when the attack actually starts and grenades are not only of great value, but are often the *only* suitable weapon which can be used. The aim is to cause surprise and to so disorientate the terrorists that they cannot kill or

Above: FFV 915 smoke grenade on a Swedish AK4 7.62mm rifle. It can be fired from any rifle fitted with the standard 22mm grenade launcher.

harm the hostages in the crucial few seconds as the special forces soldiers gain entry. The British SAS led the way in sponsoring the development of 'stun' grenades (also known, more prosaically, as 'flash-bangs'), which emit a sudden and extremely bright light, accompanied by a very loud, but harmless explosion, which combine to disorientate the terrorists for a few seconds.

Great precautions are taken to prevent harming innocent hostages with these stun grenades; the latest British types have an expelling charge which

Above: The Soviet AGS-17 automatic grenade launcher nicknamed Plamya (Flame). It has an effective range of 875-1, 312yd (800-1,200m). The drum magazine contains 30-rounds.

Left: Haley & Weller E182 multi-burst stun grenade uses the H&W patented silent electrical ignition system; the lever does not leave the grenade, nor is there any sound of a cap firing.

blows the metal igniter set off immediately after leaving the thrower's hand, and a cardboard body for the main charge; thus, no metal components can cause injury on explosion of the charge. The Royal Ordnance G60/09 has a rubber, fully water-proof body, just 2.44in (62mm) in diameter and 3.93in (100mm) in length, weighing 7oz (200g); it fits very neatly into a man's hand and is easy to conceal. On detonation it throws out seven charges which explode emitting sound greater than 160dB with a light intensity of 3 million candelas. Grenades with a single charge can have a louder and brighter effect; for example, the Brock XFS-1 has a peak noise level of 180dB at 3ft (1m) and emits a flash with an intensity of 50 million candelas.

OVER THE past 20 years, as the operations carried out by revolutionaries and terrorists have intensified, so their weapons and equipment have become more sophisticated and up-to-date. One of the countermeasures taken by, if not forced upon, the security forces — who are constrained by legal factors which their enemies can safely ignore — has been an increasing use of high technology, not only to introduce new techniques, but also to refine old ideas. Indeed, many items of weaponry and military equipment which just two or three decades ago would have been thought positively medieval, are now not only in use but are also being updated by the application of modern technology. Thus, body armor, protective helmets with visors, shields, cross-bows, maces and knives all have their place in the modern armory.

The cross-bow is an old weapon undergoing something of a revival, although it has attracted some adverse publicity due to its use by common criminals in armed robberies in various countries. It is a very effective and highly accurate weapon firing a powerful bolt over ranges up to about 150yd (137m). It has two principal advantages: it is virtually silent, and its small size and light weight make it easy to carry and conceal. Modern cross-bows are made of carefully chosen materials combining great strength with lightness, use telescopic sights and are very accurate. They are certainly used by French special forces and probably by others, as well.

The whole area of combat knives has also been re-examined to produce much more effective devices, usually capable of many tasks in addition to their traditional purposes. Modern bayonets, for example, are increasingly useful, not only designed to be effective both as bayonets and as stabbing knives, but also for other purposes such as wire-cutting and can-opening.

One of the most dangerous situations for units involved in anti-riot duties occurs if the rioters get too close. Numerous

Above: As terrorists become more sophisticated special forces have started to use helmets with all-round head and neck protection.

Left: Special forces have led development of the humble bayonet into a multi-purpose tool. This Soviet bayonet is also a saw and a wire-cutter.

weapons have been produced to restore the stand-off in a melée situation, one of which is the US-produced Power-Staf KA-1. This hand-held device consists of a piston with a load-spreading impact tip, a high-pressure air control system and a compressed-air cylinder. When the trigger is pressed, air pressure forces the piston forward at a speed of some 26f/s (7.5m/s); as it.reaches its full extension of 1.5ft (457mm) the cylinder immediately retracts, the complete cycle taking some 82ms. One load of compressed

Below: An SF soldier has a helmet and respirator with built-in radio, and a pressel switch within easy reach on his chest for instant communications.

air is sufficient for some 32 cycles. The Power-Staf is thus a means of producing a series of powerful physical blows to opponents at close quarters and is a modern equivalent of the medieval mace.

A casemate was a moveable shelter used to protect individual sappers as they moved forward near the foot of castle walls in an olden-time siege. This idea, too, has been updated by the Belgian firm Fabrique Nationale (FN) which produces a series of wheeled shelters constructed of armor plate, which are used to

Below: Dressed for operations a special forces soldier wears modern body armor, both more effective and easier to wear than that in use ten years ago.

shelter EOD (explosive ordnance disposal) men as they inch forward to inspect suspected explosive devices.

Shields can be invaluable, not only for protection against missiles hurled by rioters, but also in hostage rescue operations to provide a degree of protection against pistol and SMG rounds, especially at the moment of entry to a house or a room. Some shields are designed for police use in riot situations; these are light in weight, frequently transparent, and provide protection against bricks, stones and other missiles.

Shields made of special materials, such as Kevlar, can, however, provide much greater protection. The British Armourshield Ballistic Protection Shield, for example, which is made of the company's own patented material, can stop short bursts from the 9mm Sterling SMG at a range of 10ft (3m).

Visually, one of the more striking developments has been the return of body armor. With hindsight it can be seen that the infantry soldiers of World Wars I and II were given far less protection than they could have had — and deserved. Indeed, the only gesture of protection was the steel helmet, although some form of body armor was occasionally used in World War I. As recently as 1954 the French artillerymen at the Battle of Dien Bien Phu were denied US 'flak jackets' despite their heavy losses from Viet Minh counter-battery fire, as this was considered contrary to a manly image!

Today, however, there is a vast range of body armor available based on the thoroughly reasonable principle that, quite apart from the humanitarian and morale aspects, it is better to give the highly skilled and expensively trained man some protection than to lose him and have to train another. The body armor available ranges from individual items designed to protect a specific part of the body to complete suits, protecting the entire body. Of course, there is a price to be paid: the more complete the protection the more cumbersome the outfit, imposing limitations on the wearer's mobility, endurance, agility and, in certain cases, vision.

The most vulnerable parts of the body are the back and chest. A vast range of items are available known variously as flak jackets, vests, waistcoats, etc, but all designed to provide specified protection for that part of the body containing the vital organs, from the neck down to the genitals, although not all jackets protect the entire area. Such protective vests are today worn not just by soldiers and policemen, but also by businessmen, diplomats and politicians, and President Sadat of Egypt's sudden apparent weight-gain during his epic visit to Israel was due to his wearing one of the earlier and more bulky protective vests.

Below: Special forces soldiers must be ready to fight in any environment at any time. This Canadian Special Service Force soldier has snow overclothes.

These protective vests can be optimised to defeat particular threats. The most general threat is of attack by bullets and vests come with varying degrees of effectiveness. An idea of the varieties available and their capabilities can be gained from the FN range of protective vests (see table below).

Whilst these protective vests have become lighter and less cumbersome, their weight is nevertheless not a factor to be overlooked. It is interesting to compare the weights of the FN

Below: An engineer of the US Army's SOF prepares to blow a demolition charge using an electrical detonator. His weapon is an Israeli 9mm UZI SMG.

Below: This all-purpose knife and carrying case is the type of equipment that can be found in the kit of British special forces troopers.

FN range of protective vests

Armor thickness	Weapon type	Calibers	Distance	Vest weight
0.08in (2mm	Pistol	0.22in; 7.65mm 0.38in; .45in; 9mm	9.8ft (3m)	7.9lb (3.6kg)
0.12in (3mm)	Pistol	0.22in; 7.65mm; 7.62mm Tokarev; 0.38in; .45in; 9mm	9.8ft (3m)	11.5lb
	SMG	0.45in; 9mm		(5.2kg)
	Carbine	0.30in	82ft (25m)	
0.16in (4mm)	Rifle	7.62mm Kalashnikov	16.8ft (5m)	15lb (6.8kg)
0.26in (6.5mm)	Rifle	7.62mm NATO 5.56mm NATO	16.8ft (5m)	24lb (10.9kg)

Above: Despite extra clothing and equipment SF soldiers must be able to undertake hazardous physical tasks and still be ready to fire their weapons at any time.

vests with those of the French EOD suit, which weighs a total of 35lb (16kg) (vest 21lb (9.5kg); trousers 9.9lb (4.5kg); collar 4.4lb (2kg)).

Modern special forces can use a variety of clothing, depending upon the mission. Sometimes standard military uniform may be required and on other occasions (for example, the British SAS during its Gibraltar operation in 1988) civilian clothes. But it was the SAS who relearned the old lesson that uniforms, too, can be used to intimidate the enemy. In medieval times knights' suits of armor were made larger than necessary and helmets made with fierce faceplates in order to frighten an opponent. Using the same techniques the SAS introduced their black uniform for anti-terrorist operations. This combines the necessary items, such as anti-gas respirator, with a black coverall and black gloves to give an outfit which terrorists must find truly awesome as these figures appear accompanied by flashes, bangs and explosions during the final assault. This style of uniform for such operations has been widely copied since it was first seen in public during the assault on the Iranian Embassy in London in 1981.

ALL TYPES of warfare have developed their own 'electronic battlefields' over the past 30 years and no element of the armed forces have been keener to use such modern technology to support their activities than the special forces. This especially applies in the area of sensors where electronics, optics and other more esoteric technologies can be used to detect enemies, to ascertain where they are, in what strength, how they are armed and equipped, and how they are behaving. Sensors are also used to assist friendly forces in their own movements, enabling them to see in poor visibility, sometimes even in total darkness, and to aim and fire weapons with the greatest accuracy. The area is, obviously, a very wide one; here we shall look briefly at which sensors might assist special forces in a hostage-rescue operation.

Assuming that the terrorists have holed up in a building, the first priority for the security forces is to find out where the terrorists and hostages are, how many there are of each, and what the general situation is. External observation is achieved by equipment such as binoculars, night-vision devices and the old-fashioned 'Mark One Eyeball'. There are, however, many modern devices which can be used to perform the task with greater effectiveness.

Infra-red (IR) techniques, by definition active and thus detectable, have been overtaken by image-intensification (II) and thermal-imaging (TI). II is an electronic technique for enhancing the very low levels of light present in all except total blackness (which can, in any case, only be produced artificially). Early II devices were large, heavy and clumsy, but modern equipment is much more compact: the Swedish Bofors NKJ-23, for example, is a hand-held, binocular device weighing just 5.5lb (2.5kg). Modern TV cameras can be fitted with either II or low light TV (LLTV) devices to enhance pictures taken at night or in poor visibility. Such devices are used not only by the military and police forces, but are also now available to commercial TV companies for news cameras.

TI is a technique by which radiated or reflected heat is converted into a real-time picture; it is thus, in effect, a depiction of temperature differences which is presented to the human observer as a pictorial image; for example, on a cathode-ray tube (CRT). At short ranges TI devices can be used to show detail not visible to the naked eye, thus 'seeing' into

Below: Devices like this Barr & Stroud Thermal Imager are essential for surveillance. The passive IR18 sees through mist, smoke and shadow.

Above: Rigid borescopes can be used to observe through apparently solid objects. Direct viewing is possible; or cameras can be attached.

windows and shadows, and past floodlights. The British Barr & Stroud IR18, for example, weighs 14.33lb (6.5kg) complete, can see to greater ranges than image intensifiers or low light TVs, can be coupled to virtually any telescope or periscope, and produces an output for any suitable 625-line TV monitor.

Borescopes use fibreoptics and were originally designed for industrial and medical purposes to see inside objects not otherwise visible to the human eye. Medical borescopes are so small and flexible that they can be inserted into arteries, giving doctors an unprecedented ability to see within the human body. In an anti-terrorist operation borescopes can be used to see 'through' objects such as walls and doors, and to look inside suspected objects such as barrels, envelopes, petrol tanks and cavities. The borescope is inserted through a very small hole and the output can be either presented to the naked eye, a camera or a TV monitor. Resolution is excellent (depending upon the lens fitted) and the device can be used to count people in a room, identify them, count and identify weapons, and assess the general situation. It is reported that they were used in the SAS operation at the Iranian Embassy.

Obviously, any communications systems used by the terrorists to contact external agencies such as 'higher controls' will be monitored and attempts will also be made to listen in on conversations within the target house. Radios and telephones can be monitored by standard means, whilst the internal conversations are monitored by devices placed on windows, walls, floors or ceilings.

Finally, in an attack on a terrorist stronghold special forces often use face-mounted night vision goggles. Secured to the soldier's head by straps these can be very light (less than 2lb (0.9kg)) and, using II techniques, can provide that small edge over the terrorists in the vital few minutes of the assault which means that the special forces will survive. However, even the most advanced night vision devices are currently of limited effectiveness in a blacked-out building; some small amount of ambient light is needed to enable them to function effectively.

SPECIAL forces have unique communications requirements due to their special roles and the command links that are associated with them. Many special operations, such as the release of hostages, are politically extremely delicate and as a result they are directed in some detail from the very highest government levels. This creates something of a communications problem within the national territory, but is even more difficult when the force is deployed into a foreign country at some distance from its homeland, such as, for example, the West German GSG-9 at Mogadishu and the US Delta Force on the Iranian operation to rescue the Embassy hostages.

Strategic communications must be secure, rapid and reliable to provide two-way communications between the deployed force commander and the political minister responsible for the direction of the operation, who will usually be located in a specially equipped crisis-management center. The latter

requires regular, accurate and timely updating on events on the ground so that, in combination with other inputs, decisions can be made and quickly promulgated.

Within the deployed force there is a requirement for rapid communications down to the lowest level, in many cases not just to team leaders, but also to every individual soldier. These radios should, if possible, be secure, since many modern terrorists have a monitoring capability. However, modern techniques enable this to be achieved without too much difficulty. The old-fashioned 'scrambler' has long been overtaken by much more effective modern means of on-line electronic encryption. For example, in a voice radio a pseudo-random pulse train, controlled by an operator-inserted key-setting, can be added to the digitised voice signal to encrypt it, with the reverse process taking place at the receiving set to convert the signal back to comprehensible speech.

For special forces at some distance from their base long-range ground- or sky-wave sets still have considerable importance, and the British MEL UK/PRC-319 is achieving considerable success in this field. This is an HF/VHF tactical radio covering the frequency band 1.5-40MHz. Very light in weight for the facilities it provides it is easily manpacked, comprising four units: a transmitter/receiver unit; an electronic message unit (EMU); and two antenna tuners. It operates using one frequency for transmit and a separate frequency for receive, and to enhance resistance to detection does not use an intermediate frequency (IF) internally. The EMU

Left: MEL Caracol is the world's first full military specification hand-held, frequency-hopping radio. It is fully interoperable with the Jaguar series radios.

Above: The revolutionary British PRC-319 radio combines great range with highly sophisticated modes of operation, including burst transmission. It is in wide SF service.

is an alphanumeric device with built-in crypto and has a 2,000 character memory. The PRC-319 employs 'burst transmission', which means that the message to be sent is prepared by typing it into the EMU where it is electronically encrypted; then, on the operator's instruction it is sent in a very short period of time. Thus, a message which could take several minutes to send by voice or teleprinter can be sent in less than 10 seconds. This technique makes it virtually impossible for hostile forces to detect, record, jam or direction-find (DF) the transmission.

The security forces also need to listen in to the terrorists and to detect any electronic devices they may be using. This requires sophisticated monitoring equipment covering as broad a segment of the electromagnetic frequency band as possible. Such equipment is essentially similar to the 'detector vans' used to discover unlicensed domestic TV receivers in the United Kingdom. It can pinpoint the location of target devices operated by illegal organisations quickly, reliably and with considerable accuracy.

The security forces can also use electronic devices to disrupt terrorist communications by jamming. This is ideally done using 'spot' jamming on a specific frequency, since this can be done with great accuracy and thus not disrupt other communications systems using adjacent frequencies.

There is a host of modern jammers available, ranging from large, multi-capable devices to very small unattended, expendable jammers, which can be placed by hand near to the target transmitter, especially in anti-terrorist operations. A typical expendable device (Racal RJS3140) weighs 2.5kg (including batteries), has an operating life of at least 120 minutes, can be set to any frequency in the band 20-90MHz, to cover a bandwidth selectable between 1 and 31MHz, and can be programmed to switch on at a specified time. Such a device would be ideal for use in jamming terrorist communications in the period immediately prior to an attack. However, few terrorists are so unsophisticated in this increasingly electronic age as to stick to one frequency and may even soon use frequency-hopping sets. Such sets are best attacked using a wide-band jammer very close by.

THE STANDARD range of military vehicles is, of course, available to special forces. All modern armies are highly dependent upon wheeled field cars, which are usually simple in construction, fast and adaptable. This makes them very suitable for use by special forces, who, not unnaturally, have some highly specialised requirements. Soon to be the most widely used vehicles among Western forces will be the US HMMWV (Hummer). Some idea of the scale of use is given by the *initial* orders for the US forces alone: 40,000 for the Army, 14,000 for the USMC and 11,000 for the USAF! Doubtless, many specialised versions will end up with US Special Operations Forces (SOF).

The British Land-Rover has been in production since 1948 and has appeared in more versions than almost any other military vehicle. A recent special forces version is based on the Rover 110 chassis and is described (somewhat euphemistically) as a 'remote-area patrol vehicle'. This open-top vehicle has a crew of three: commander, driver and gunner. The commander's seat is next to the driver and is raised slightly, while the gunner sits on a special mount in the rear of the vehicle. Armament is varied according to customers' requirements, but typically comprises a 7.62mm GPMG pintle-mounting in front of the commander and a single or twin mounting for two 7.62mm GPMGs, 0.50in Brownings or 7.62mm Chain Guns on the gunner's mounting.

In the USA the design of the Californian 'Dune-Buggy' used by rich young people as a 'fun-car' on the Pacific beaches has been developed into the Fast Attack Vehicle (FAV) (also known as the 'Scorpion'). This vehicle has no bodywork as such, is very low-slung in design and is powered by an air-cooled, 94hp Volkswagen engine. It has 4 × 2 drive, but its exceptionally high power to weight ratio gives it superb cross-country performance, with a top speed of 80mph (128km/h). A large variety of weapons fits is possible. A similar vehicle, the Engesa EE-VAR, has been developed in Brazil. This is a two-seater and is also powered by a Volkswagen air-cooled engine; it can mount

Below: One of the vehicles used by US Special Forces is the new standard field car, the HMMWV (Hummer) fitted with special-to-role equipment.

Above: The Emerson Fast Attack Vehicle (FAV) used by US Special Forces. A two-man vehicle, it can be fitted with many types of weapon to suit mission requirements.

Below: FAV in scrub country. Such vehicles are used in low-threat areas in missions requiring high cross-country mobility, high speed and heavy firepower.

7.62mm or 0.5in machine guns, 40mm mortars or TOW ATGWs.

Special forces also have a great interest in special versions of normal civilian vehicles, particularly those with enhanced protection for use in urban environments. Thus, they use apparently standard civilian cars and vans, which have armored protection, special tyres and custom-built communications fits. These are used for surveillance or moving VIPs. For larger groups armored buses are used, which provide a self-contained, comfortable place in which to wait, complete with communications and other facilities.

OTHER SUPER-VALUE MILITARY GUIDES IN THIS SERIES......

Air War over Vietnam
Allied Fighters of World War II
Battleships and Battlecruisers
Bombers of World War II
Electronic Warfare
German, Italian and Japanese Fighters
  of World War II
Israeli Air Force
Military Helicopters
Modern Airborne Missiles
Modern American Fighters
Modern Destroyers
Modern Elite Forces
Modern Fighters and Attack Aircraft
Modern Soviet Air Force

Modern Soviet Ground Forces
Modern Soviet Navy
Modern Sub Hunters
Modern Submarines
Modern Tanks
Modern US Air Force
Modern US Army
Modern US Navy
Modern Warships
NATO Fighters
Pistols and Revolvers
Rifles and Sub-machine Guns
Space Warfare
Strategic Weapons
World War II Tanks

✱ Each is colourfully illustrated with hundreds of action photos and technical drawings
✱ Each contains concisely presented data and accurate descriptions of major international weapons
✱ Each represents tremendous value

If you would like further information on any of our titles please write to:
Publicity Dept. (Military Div.), Salamander Books Ltd.,
52 Bedford Row, London WC1R 4LR